THE
BELIEVING
HEART

THE BELIEVING HEART

NOURISHING THE
SEED OF FAITH
Second Edition

BRUCE C. HAFEN

Deseret Book Company
Salt Lake City, Utah

Library of Congress Cataloging-in-Publication Data

Hafen, Bruce C.
   The believing heart / by Bruce C. Hafen.
     p.   cm.
   Includes bibliographical references and index.
   Contents: The believing heart—If with all your heart—The
value of the veil—On dealing with uncertainty—Their arm shall
be my arm—When do the angels come?
   ISBN 0-87579-419-X (hard)
   ISBN 1-57345-107-X (paper)
   1. Christian life—Mormon authors.   I. Title.
BX8656.H34   1990
248.4'89332—dc20   90-43781
                                                CIP

Printed in the United States of America   18961

10 9 8 7 6 5 4 3 2 1

To the prophet Alma,
who taught us that a testimony is a
living, growing thing;
and that faith is a process, not an event.

Contents

Preface to the Second Edition

Since 1971, I have been blessed to teach religion, law, and the liberal arts at Brigham Young University and at Ricks College. I have loved this teaching experience, because it has created uplifting associations with curious and believing young people, and because it has permitted me to explore my own questions about life in an atmosphere of faith.

During the early 1980s, I began collecting my teaching notes and my personal study notes in an effort to define the three religious issues that, by then, held the greatest meaning for me—faith, the Atonement of Jesus Christ, and relationships among people. I noticed, gradually, some strong developmental connections among these three topics: (1) faith prepares us to receive the Atonement; (2) the Atonement purifies, mellows, and strengthens us; and (3) the Atonement then helps us build our relationships with the Lord and with others, especially family members.

Mormon has eloquently described this developmental process: "And the first fruits of repentance is baptism; and baptism cometh by faith unto the fulfilling the commandments; and the fulfilling the commandments bringeth remission of sins; And the remission of sins bringeth meekness, and lowliness of heart; and because of meekness and lowliness of heart cometh the visitation of the Holy Ghost, which Comforter filleth with hope and perfect love, which love endureth by diligence unto prayer, until the end shall come, when all the saints shall dwell with God." (Moroni 8:25–26.)

In a conversation in about 1984, Marie — my wife and my closest spiritual and intellectual confidante — and I first entertained the thought of some day preparing a series of three books that would push us to clarify what we were learning about these three interconnected themes. The possible titles seemed very natural: *The Believing Heart, The Broken Heart,* and *The Belonging Heart.* We saw the third volume as a project we might work on as co-authors. That is a hope we still nurture.

With notes and assorted rough sketches scattered about on pieces of all three topics, but with too much else to do, we decided to wait for quieter years to work on our "trilogy of the heart." Then Cory Maxwell from Bookcraft nudged me to the point of preparing four essays on faith as the first edition of *The Believing Heart* in 1986.

In 1988, Stanley A. Peterson of the Church Educational System invited me to speak about the Atonement to the Church's seminary and institute teachers at their annual summer symposium at BYU. Because of what I knew I would learn from the remarkable "peer review" process the symposium provided, this struck me as a unique opportunity to pull together the partly incoherent fragments I had been collecting on that topic. Sheri Dew of Deseret Book Company later ran across a copy of this symposium talk, and she urged that it become the basis for *The Broken Heart,* which Deseret subsequently published in 1989.

In the meantime, Bookcraft's first printing of *The Be-lieving Heart* expired, and Deseret Book acquired the copyright from Bookcraft with the thought of publishing a revised and enlarged second edition as a companion volume to *The Broken Heart*. This book is the result of that process. I have reworked the first four chapters somewhat and have added two new chapters, the seeds of which were scattered through those files from the past.

Chapter one, "The Believing Heart," is less fully developed than the rest of the book, because it only introduces themes that are more naturally developed in later chapters.

Quotations from Alma's memorable allegory on the seed of faith in Alma 32 introduce each chapter. When I began my missionary service as a young man, Alma 32 was my anchor, as my testimony was only beginning to take root. Because of inexperience, I felt very green; yet someone assured me that only green things grow. The idea that religious faith develops through a process of growth — like a living, growing tree — increasingly rang true with my experience.

In those days, I thought Alma was speaking about faith in God in the most basic and general sense. But now I see that the seed and the tree also convey a more specialized and, hence, a more potent message, a message I suppose we will begin to grasp only "after the trial of [our] faith." (See Ether 12:6.) Through the learning process of completing *The Broken Heart*, I began to see how powerfully the seed of faith is connected to the doctrine of the Atonement.

Alma taught his masterful lesson on faith to a group of impoverished Zoramites. He taught them the process by which the seed may, if properly nourished, grow *within them* into "a tree springing up unto everlasting life." The fruit of this tree is "most precious," "sweet above all that is sweet," "white above all that is white, yea, and pure above all that is pure; and ye shall feast upon this fruit even until ye are filled, that ye hunger not, neither shall ye thirst." (Alma 32:41–42.)

This tree is the same tree of life described in the story of Adam and Eve (see Genesis 1–3). The fruit of this tree is depicted in Lehi's dream as "the most desirable above all things" and "the most joyous to the soul." (1 Nephi 11:22–23.) In a general sense, the tree of life represents the "love of God" (1 Nephi 11:22), but in a more focused theological sense, God's love as symbolized by this tree is most fully expressed in the Atonement of Jesus Christ.

After Alma concluded his sermon on the seed and the tree, his listeners were receptive enough to ask "how they should plant the seed, or the word of which he had spoken, which he said must be planted in their hearts; or in what manner they should exercise their faith." (Alma 33:1.) Alma concluded his answer to these questions with a moving invitation for his audience to keep their eyes on the holy Atonement of the Son of God, a life-giving tree whose fruit would bless them not only with forgiveness of sin, but also with the strength to bear all of life's burdens and, finally, with the capacity to enter into the Lord's rest through the "joy" that is in Christ:

> [C]ast about your eyes and begin to believe in the Son of God, that he will come to redeem his people, and that he shall suffer and die to atone for their sins; and that he shall rise again from the dead, which shall bring to pass the resurrection, that all men shall stand before him, to be judged at the last and judgment day, according to their works.

And now, my brethren, I desire that ye shall plant *this word* [the Atonement] in your hearts, and as it beginneth to swell even so nourish it by your faith. And behold, it will become a tree, springing up in you unto everlasting life. And *then may God grant unto you that your burdens may be light, through the joy of his Son.* And even all this can ye do if ye will. Amen. (Alma 33:22–23; emphasis added.)

The tree of life waits for us, as it did for Adam and Eve, Lehi and Sariah, at the end of the inviting, but sometimes treacherous and lonely, path of faith. The way of that path is clearly marked by the iron rod of God's word. We take our first steps (and many later ones) along this path through our freely chosen desire to have a believing heart—for "even all this can ye do *if ye will.*"

Provo, Utah
August 1990

The Believing Heart

Yea, even if ye can no more than desire to believe, let this desire work in you . . . that a seed may be planted in your heart.

(Alma 32:27–28.)

One late summer after-
noon when our family was visiting relatives in a large and
distant city, our four-year-old son suddenly disappeared
from a city park. We all began a search of the area, ultimately involving the police as well as many neighbors.
After about two hours, darkness came and we still had
not found our boy. Our concern changed to real worry.

Finally, we gathered our family together and with a
solemnity that is rare among children, we knelt in prayer.
A short time later the city police telephoned to report
that they had found our son, almost precisely as we had
requested in the prayer. Before long, a police car drove
up to the house, its precious cargo a bit shaken, but intact.

Later that night before he dropped off to sleep, the
boy's six-year-old brother said to me, as he reflected on
what had happened, "Dad, you're kind of magic, sort of,
aren't you?" I replied that what we'd seen was not magic —
the Lord had simply answered our prayers.

Would our son have turned up anyway? I don't know;
but our family chooses to believe that the prayer made
a difference.

A few years ago, a university student related to his
elders' quorum an event he had experienced just after
being ordained a deacon in the Aaronic Priesthood. He
lived on a farm, and his father had promised him that an

expected new calf would be his very own to raise. One summer morning when his parents were away, he was working in the barn when the pregnant cow began to calve prematurely. He watched in great amazement as the little calf was born, and then, without warning, the mother cow suddenly rolled over the calf. She was trying to kill it. In his heart he cried out to the Lord for help. Not thinking about how much more the cow weighed than he did, he pushed on her with all his strength and somehow moved her away.

He picked up the lifeless calf in his arms and, brokenhearted, looked at it, the tears running down his cheeks. Then he remembered that he now held the priesthood, and he felt he had every right to pray for additional help. So he prayed from the depths of his boyish, believing heart. Before long the little animal began breathing again. The young deacon knew his prayer had been heard.

After he finished telling this story, the tears welled up in his eyes and he said, "Brethren, I shared that experience because I don't think I would do now what I did then. Now that I am older, less naive, and more experienced, I 'know better' than to expect help in that kind of situation. I am not sure I would believe now, even if I relived that experience, that the calf's survival was anything more than a coincidence. I don't understand what has happened to me since that time, but I wonder if something is missing now."

Whatever his change in attitude was, I also wondered about it. Did it matter? He was a faithful Church member and a good person. But he had become less childlike, less believing. Was he simply more mature now, or had his sense of the miraculous waned?

We live in sophisticated times. We are naturally inclined to regard what might be a genuine spiritual experience as a coincidence, unless there is conclusive evidence that spiritual forces were indeed involved. However, we are sometimes required to make decisions that require action before compelling proof is available.

As developed more fully in chapter three, the scriptures teach that God deliberately, and for wise purposes, uses restraint in manifesting himself to us. Yet, paradoxically, he remains deeply interested and involved in our lives. Because of his restraint in the midst of such interest, we must learn to perceive the hand of the Lord in situations where his presence may be still and small. Our willingness to "be believing" helps make such perception possible.

The risen Lord counseled the Apostle Thomas to "reach hither thy hand and thrust it into my side: and be not faithless, but believing." (John 20:27.) Moroni, speaking to our generation, said: "And who shall say that Jesus Christ did not many mighty miracles? . . . and he ceaseth not to be God, and is a God of miracles. . . . Doubt not, but be believing." (Mormon 9:18–19, 27.) Similarly, the Lord said: "Search diligently, pray always, and be believing, and all things shall work together for your good, if ye walk uprightly." (D&C 90:24.)

The act of believing originates in the heart of the beholder through his or her voluntary action. (See chapter five.) On more than one occasion the Lord said to those around him, "He that hath ears to hear, let him hear." (Luke 8:8.) Few of those who observed him truly understood the parables or perceived the miracles for what they were.

It is not always easy to know at first which influences are of divine origin. Those who first heard about the

Savior's healings faced this question just as we do today when we hear the testimony of a miraculous healing. Was it really a miracle, or would the person have recovered anyway? Did the Lord really help us find our boy? Did the calf really receive some new infusion of life in answer to a boy's prayer? In the early history of the Salt Lake Valley, were the seagulls really sent to take away the crickets?

Even the matter of God's existence can appear to be a close question. Some argue that with all the misery of life, there couldn't be a God; others say that the obvious order in nature could never have been accidental. Neither side seems to persuade the other on the basis of external evidence.

It just might be that the Lord planned it that way — so we are not forced by the circumstances to believe. There are so many things he could do to rend the veil. But "we walk by faith, not by sight." (2 Corinthians 5:7.)

Scholars in the philosophy of knowledge tell us that people tend to see what they want to see, especially when the evidence is ambiguous. Perhaps that is why the mists of darkness in Lehi's dream are so descriptive of the conditions of mortality. God has chosen to leave us free, amid circumstances that do not compel our belief. Here we may determine for ourselves, as an act of will, whether to grasp the iron rod in the midst of the mortal darkness. All four of Lehi's sons were born of those same "goodly parents." (1 Nephi 1:1.) The difference between the believers (Nephi and Sam) and the unbelievers (Laman and Lemuel) was not so much in what happened to them, but in their *attitude* toward what happened. That attitude originated within their own hearts, with each making his own free choice about being willing to be believing.

Certainly Christ might have been born under circumstances so overwhelming and miraculous that all who lived at the time of his birth could not have questioned his supernatural origin. But he came more quietly than that, a light that "shineth in the darkness; and the darkness comprehended it not. . . . But as many as *received him,* to them gave he power to become the sons of God, even to them that believe on his name." (John 1:5, 12; italics added.)

It was all part of a plan carefully and deliberately designed *not* to *compel* belief. Further indications of the deliberateness of that plan appear throughout the accounts of the Savior's life. Frequently he told those who were blessed by a miracle that they "should tell no man what was done." (Luke 8:56; see also Matthew 8:4.)

One essential element in that plan is the principle of "line upon line, precept upon precept." Not only does he leave to us the initiative to believe, he also imparts to his hearers only what they are ready to hear. Milk comes before meat. "I have yet many things to say unto you, but ye cannot bear them now." (John 16:12.)

Said the Lord to Joseph Smith after revealing to him the words spoken to Moses on the mountain: "See thou show [these words] unto no man, until I command you, except to them that believe." (Moses 4:32.)

Hugh Nibley has described this guiding principle as the "policy of reticence," which the Lord has always followed "to protect sacred things from common misunderstandings and to protect the unworthy from damaging themselves with them."[1]

The Lord has also made it plain that it is not good to seek signs. (See Matthew 12:39; Mark 8:12.) Moreover, miracles are not proof of divine authority. Satan can also work wonders so marvelous "that, if it were possible, they shall deceive the very elect." (Matthew 24:24.) Apparently, there is a profound difference between the person "that saith unto me, Lord, Lord," and the person who "*doeth the will of my Father* which is in heaven." (Matthew 7:21; emphasis added.)

A key reason for the Lord's unwillingness to compel our belief is suggested by those scriptural phrases about doing the will of the Father and "receiving him." Something happens to people who receive him—who do his will. They learn. They develop Christlike capacities and skills beyond the reach of other people. Following his will changes them. These changes do not occur within the lives of those who merely see the sign or hear the word. Such changes in character and spirit also do not happen without our active, voluntary participation. Thus, by being believing, by receiving the Lord, and by following him, the process of becoming *like him* is set into motion. That is a point he does not want us to miss.

Knowing these reasons for the Lord's restraint should make us less inclined to wait for irrefutable evidence before we will act like believers. The Lord is not likely to make the case miraculously irresistible. That would be contrary to the purpose of mortality, because it would inhibit the growth and development that a free environment is designed to permit.

If, then, it is not good to seek signs and wonders, some may ask why the Lord performed the great miracles of his earthly ministry. Why the wonders of Moses' time? If the Lord had the power to send the seagulls, why didn't he keep the crickets away in the first place?

One reason is revealed in the Lord's answer when

Moses asked why He had performed such great wonders when He freed Israel from captivity: "that thou mayest tell in the ears of thy son, and of thy son's son, what things I have wrought in Egypt, and my signs which I have done among them; that ye may know how that I am the Lord." (Exodus 10:2.) I think of that passage when I see the seagull monument on Temple Square, and we have tried to tell our children what the monument stands for.

The Lord wants us to know, if we have ears to hear, that we are finally and ultimately dependent upon him. The great miracles are symbolic of the way the Savior's atonement intervenes in our lives as a pure act of grace, offering redemption "after all we can do." (See 2 Nephi 25:23.) In the wilderness of our own experience, whenever that may be for each of us, we will at some time and in some way confront that total dependence, as did the children of Israel standing before the waters of the Red Sea.

And yet, paradoxically, even that confrontation is not likely to be overwhelming, lest we be deprived of the very experiences intended to be produced by that wilderness and the free agency that accompanies it.

The Lord has used the highly visible forms of his power very sparingly—enough to leave us with clear witnesses, but not enough to compel us to believe.

Once the conduct of a person's life has shown that he is indeed a believer, the signs of divine influence will follow him, in part as a further witness, but primarily to bless others.

What a careful balance has been struck between too much and not enough in the manifestations of divine power! How essential, then, to be willing to recognize the quiet evidences for what they are.

If we are willing to see miracles, what should we look for? Elder James E. Talmage wrote that miracles have been broadly classified as phenomena that are "unusual, special, transitory, and wrought by an agency beyond the power of man's control."[2] But in our sophisticated and complex day, few things that happen, large or small, seem to be beyond man's control.

As we have begun to understand how technological miracles operate, our tendency to ascribe what we don't understand to supernatural origins has declined. Elder Talmage wrote, "The human sense of the miraculous wanes as comprehension of the operative process increases."[3] Having watched men walk on the moon, we are quite comfortable with wonders, so much so that even when we haven't any idea how some marvelous thing could happen — like the new cure of a dreaded disease — we assume that some expert somewhere understands how it happened. Thus, we are left stripped of a sense of wonder. Whatever it is, thinks the contemporary mind, there is some natural explanation for it.

Perhaps, in view of this modern-day tendency, we need to think of miracles not as all the phenomena we can't understand, but simply as the influence of divine forces. In a broad sense, divine forces are involved in all nature and all technology. But if the Lord is directly involved in our personal affairs, that is a special miracle, however quiet, however common it may be. Does God want us to be able to recognize that kind of miracle? Yes. "And in nothing doth man offend God, or against none is his wrath kindled, save those who confess not his hand in all things, and obey not his commandments." (D&C 59:21.)

Why would he be concerned that we recognize his influence? It can't be just to satisfy his need for recognition.

We know too much about his character and attributes to take that possibility seriously. It must have something to do with us — with whether we receive him, with whether we become like him. If his hand touches the circumstances of our lives, and we affirmatively reach out to take his hand, we can be guided toward those experiences uniquely suited to further our personal development of a Christlike character. Thereby will we understand the meaning of "be believing, and all things shall work together for your good." (D&C 90:24.)

God is so close, so available to those who have ears to hear and eyes to see. In Jacob's dream about the ladder reaching to heaven, with angels ascending and descending it, he saw God standing at the top of the ladder saying, "I am with thee, and will keep thee in all places whither thou goest." And then Jacob awoke and said, "Surely the Lord is in this place: and I knew it not." (See Genesis 28:13–16.) President Harold B. Lee used to say, "Our Lord is not an absentee father. He is closer to the leaders of this church than you have any idea." He is also closer to us individually than most of us have any idea. The Lord is here, and who knows it? The faithful, those who are willing to be believing, because their greatest desire is to find him and serve him. When he is there, they know it.

All this is not intended to imply that we should be overzealous in looking for the Lord's hand, nor should it imply that God is so involved in human affairs that we are relieved of either our freedom or our responsibility in life. But it does imply that he may well be more involved in our lives than many suppose. Interestingly, the nature of that involvement probably means more, not less, for both our freedom and our responsibility.

10

So, what kinds of quiet miracles do believers perceive, from which they derive strength, assurance, and spiritual growth?

One example is "the awesome, sobering miracle of the newborn babe—with hands reaching, with eyes watching, with ears listening, and intelligence that responds to truth. . . .Who gave two cells the intelligence to join and divide, to become an eye, or a tooth, or the hair of the head? . . . Surely immortality is no more a miracle than mortality is."[4]

Another example is to see a grown man cry, when, after years of neglecting his children and his wife, the Spirit penetrates his heart; and he changes—his interests, his allegiance, his countenance, his conduct.

Also, to walk through the valley of evil, and, after coming to oneself, to feel with Alma "that the very thought of coming into the presence of my God did rack my soul with inexpressible horror." (Alma 36:14.) And then, after much anguish, to finally understand what it means to have a Savior. In Alma's words, "And oh, what joy, and what marvelous light I did behold: yea, my soul was filled with joy as exceeding as was my pain!" (Alma 36:20.) As those who hear the confessions of the truly repentant know, there are many among us who reach that understanding with everlasting gratitude for a life-changing process that naturalistic terms cannot fully explain. That is the miracle of forgiveness.

A further illustration of how the believing heart responds is *The Windows of Heaven*, the historical film-story of a modern-day prophet's inspired promise to his people that if they would pay their tithing an awful drought would come to an end. There we see a faithful farmer and his faithful wife, after the planting, the waiting, the watching, and the thirsting, falling to their knees in gratitude in the parched red soil as finally the rains come, pouring down upon their bowed heads.

And then we see President Lorenzo Snow receive a telegram in his office, telling of the rain; and we see him instinctively hasten to kneel at his bedside and say something like, "Oh, what can I do to show my gratitude that thou hast heard the prayers of thy people and thy humble servant? I would give anything, even my life."

Neither that prophet nor those farmers stood by, watching the rain, wondering if perhaps it was just a coincidence. Their attitudes, their experiences, and their instincts told them otherwise. They knew in whom they had trusted.

It should be added that the way people live has much, perhaps everything, to do with how even the still, small miracles influence their lives. "And there was not any man who could do a miracle in the name of Jesus save he were cleansed every whit from his iniquity." (3 Nephi 8:1.) Living up to that condition provides an incentive for righteous living that mere sign-seeking cannot offer.

Moreover, a believing attitude affects not only how we think, but also what we *do* in response to our religious commitments. The genuine expectation that God will keep his promises makes the believing heart also a faithful heart. In this way, belief leads to action.

There is an analogy here between "investing" in our relationship with the Lord and investing in economic and human relationships. The emerging collapse of communistic economic systems validates Jeremy Bentham's explanation of why private ownership of property is more economically productive than collective ownership: the human motivations that result in economic production simply do not operate fully in the absence of secure expectations about future enjoyment of the fruits of our labors. The will to labor and the will to invest depend on stable rules that assure people they will be allowed to enjoy the products of both their labor and the savings they have risked. Economic systems based on private ownership are premised on those stable rules, while systems of collective ownership are not. Therefore, as recent history demonstrates, collective systems simply cannot be economically competitive, over time, with private systems.

For the same reason, couples who view marriage as a permanent relationship will "invest" far more completely in the relationship than do couples who merely live together temporarily, perhaps waiting to see if the relationship "works out." Those living in a noncommittal, short-term relationship will not invest themselves in the relationship emotionally, financially, or otherwise, because they lack a reasonable belief that the likelihood of future benefits justifies the inconvenience and the self-sacrifice required in relationships of real commitment. Therefore, the skepticism implied by a "non-binding commitment" (a classic oxymoron) becomes a self-fulfilling prophecy, because without the voluntary investment of energy, time, and self-restraint, the noncommittal relationship really *cannot* bear the fruits of enduring mutual support.

So it is in our relationship with the Lord. His is a stable system that assures a guaranteed return on our investments. "I the Lord am bound when ye do what I say." (D&C 82:10.) As a friend once said to me with a knowing wink, "Of course the Lord will bless you. That's his *job*."

But the fruits of faith do not "just happen." As chapter five suggests more fully, we actually help nourish the development of those fruits by acting in wholehearted reliance on our firm expectation that the Lord will keep his promises. If I believe the Lord will help me move a mountain, I fully invest my energy in starting to move it, even if only one shovel full at a time. If I believe the Lord will bless me with greater financial wisdom when I pay my tithing, I will literally "invest" in that expectation. And when the still, small voice begins to guide my other financial choices, I am more likely both to hear it and to respond to it, because I expected it to come along. When the voice of inspiration knocks at the door of our heart, we won't then ask suspiciously, "Who's there?" Rather, we may say, "Come in — I've been expecting you."

Therefore did King Benjamin teach his people. "*Believe* in God; *believe* that he is, and that he created all things. . . ; *believe* that he has all wisdom, and all power, both in heaven and in earth; . . . *believe* that ye must repent of your sins and forsake them, and humble yourselves before God; . . . *and now, if you believe all these things see that ye do them.*" (Mosiah 4:9–10; emphasis added.)

Many of us have experienced in some way the realization of our own long-awaited rainstorm, our miracle of forgiveness, our lost boy found, our seagulls come. And because of these experiences, we can say with Jacob, "Surely the Lord is in this place." (Genesis 28:16.) Or we can say with Moroni, "For the eternal purposes of the Lord shall roll on, until all his promises shall be fulfilled." (Mormon 8:22.)

Yet the real confirmation, the actual realization that he was "in this place," and that he actually fulfills his promises in our own lives, often comes later — the harvest of those early decisions to be believing. "On the good ground are they, which in an honest and good heart, having heard the word, keep it, and bring forth fruit with patience." (Luke 8:15.) After a few seasons of such harvesting, and of doing what believers do, the faithful, believing heart becomes more and more a knowing heart.

Significantly, those experiences also bring with them increased capacities of character and spirit, and thus is brought to partial fruition the greatest miracle of all — our own divine potential to become Christlike. That is a miracle nature's laws simply do not, perhaps cannot, produce without the trial of our faith. And the beginning of it all is to doubt not, but be believing. That first step and the conduct that follows it are under our exclusive, personal control.

Notes

1. Hugh Nibley, *Since Cumorah* (Salt Lake City: Deseret Book Co., 1967), page 107.
2. James E. Talmage, *Jesus the Christ* (Salt Lake City: Deseret Book Co., 1961), page 148.
3. *Jesus the Christ,* page 148.
4. Richard L. Evans, Jr., *Richard Evans: The Man and the Message* (Salt Lake City: Bookcraft, 1973), pages 130–31.

CHAPTER TWO

"If with All Your Heart"

For ye know that the word hath swelled your souls, and . . . your understanding doth begin to be enlightened, and your mind doth begin to expand. O then, is not this real?

(Alma 32:34–35.)

In Mendelssohn's oratorio *Elijah* are some songs of exquisite and tender spiritual depth. The text from one of them reads: " 'If with all your hearts ye truly seek me, ye shall ever surely find me,' Thus saith our God. Oh! that I knew where I might find Him, that I might even come before His presence! Oh! that I knew, where I might find him! 'If with all your hearts ye truly seek me; Ye shall ever surely find me.' Thus saith our God."[1]

One fall season not long ago, I found myself thinking more than usual about this song and its message, when our closely knit community experienced several unexpected deaths within the space of a few days. One of these was Don Decker, a favorite English teacher at Ricks College, who died in a climbing accident in the Teton mountains. Another was a close friend of our older children, a high school senior named Howard Pack. Howard died of a sudden heart failure during a long-distance run. It was very hard for our three teenage sons the night the news came to us. We sat up a long time that night, just crying and talking and trying to understand things we really couldn't understand.

Then we learned of the passing of Terry Crapo, an Idaho Falls lawyer and priesthood leader who also taught at the BYU law school. Terry, who was my own age, was for me what Howard Pack was for my sons — a close friend and a rare personal example. I was especially stunned at Terry's loss, partly because of our close relationship, but partly because Terry's contributions were so extraordinary that I couldn't imagine the world getting along without him. He was blessed with rich intellectual gifts and was wholehearted and childlike in his devotion to the Church. His was a believing heart.

When Terry was a BYU student, a perceptive religion teacher named West Belnap said to him, "Terry, we have many people in the Church who have it in their heads, and we have many who have it in their hearts. But we have very, very few who have it in both their heads and their hearts." Brother Belnap admonished Terry to develop his head as well as his heart and then to give both fully in the service of God and other people. Terry Crapo did just that, as well as anyone I have known.

As I sat during Terry's funeral and looked at his wife, Val, and their family sitting on the front row, my mind went back to another funeral and another family, and I found in my memory some needed reassurance. West Belnap, the teacher who touched Terry's life, also touched mine. It was in his class that my wife, Marie, and I first met. The class was called "Your Religious Problems." (We solved our most pressing religious problem by finding each other.) West Belnap, like Terry Crapo, died of cancer in his early forties. He had also served the Church with unusual skill and dedication, having been chairman of Religious Instruction at BYU and chairman of the Adult Correlation Committee for the Church.

I will long remember the talk at West's funeral given by Elder Harold B. Lee, who was then a member of the Council of the Twelve. Elder Lee had associated intimately with West in the work of the Church's correlation committees. Rather than just stating that West had been called to another assignment, Elder Lee parted the veil of his heart enough to let the congregation know of his own pain and of his own searching to understand. He looked at West's wife and eight children on the front row and said something like this: "We say he has gone on to something more important. But as we look at this sorrowing little family, our hearts want to cry out, 'What can possibly be more important than this? And who can do the work as he did it for the university and for the Church?'" He talked further about his experiences with West. Finally he said with a sober calmness, "Nevertheless, we know in whom we have trusted. We do not understand, but we do not complain. We have learned to trust the Lord, our God."

I was stirred by the candor of Elder Lee's testimony. He was so honest. He was not embarrassed to share his true feelings. He was not content with quick, superficial answers to everything. Somehow, his honest acknowledgment of what he did not know gave added strength to what he did know. That kind of testimony is real enough to be strong when the hard times come.

We see testimonies having that kind of depth in the lives of other prophets. Think of the prophet Elijah, in despair after being rejected by those he tried so hard to rescue: "It is enough; . . . O Lord, take away my life." Think of Joseph Smith in Liberty Jail: "O God, where art thou? And where is the pavilion that covereth thy hiding place?" Think even of the Savior: "If it be possible, let this cup pass from me: nevertheless not as I will, but as thou wilt." (See 1 Kings 19:4; D&C 121:1; Matthew 26:39.)

Each of these, in his turn, was faithful to the end. It

is as if each had his moment to wonder, "Oh! that I knew where I might find my Lord." Yet each sought him with all his heart, until surely he did find him.

Our Father in Heaven wants to help us develop testimonies strong enough to withstand any kind of pressure, any kind of pain or adversity—testimonies strong enough to return us to his presence. As Joseph Smith wrote:

> For a man to lay down his all, his character and reputation, . . . his houses, his lands, . . . his wife and children, and even his own life . . . requires more than mere belief or supposition that he is doing the will of God; but actual knowledge, realizing that, when these sufferings are ended, he will enter into eternal rest, and be a partaker of the glory of God.
>
> A religion that does not require the sacrifice of all things never has power sufficient to produce the faith necessary unto life and salvation; . . . It is through the medium of the sacrifice of all earthly things that men do actually know that they are well pleasing in the sight of God.[2]

Someone once said you can't visually tell the difference between a strand of cobweb and a strand of powerful cable—until stress is put on the strand. Our testimonies are that way, and for most of us, the days of stress for our testimonies have already begun. It may not be the death of a loved one. We might not yet have been asked to give up something that is really precious to us, though the time for such a test may well come to us by and by. Our current stress is more likely to come in the form of overpowering temptations, which show us that a shallow acceptance of the gospel does not have the power to cope with the full fury of the powers of darkness. Perhaps there is a mission call to a place of illness and disappointment, when we had planned on a mission to a place of unbounded opportunity. Or perhaps there are too many questions to which our limited knowledge simply has no answer, and those who claim to know more than we do taunt us with what appears to be a persuasive certainty.

When those times come, our testimonies must be more than the cobweb strands of a fair-weather faith. They need to be like strands of cable, powerful enough to resist the shafts of him who would destroy us. In our days of stress and trouble, we must be built "upon the rock of our Redeemer, who is Christ, the Son of God, ... that when the devil shall send forth his mighty winds, yea, his shafts in the whirlwind, ... and his mighty storm shall beat upon you, it shall have no power over you, ... because of the rock upon which ye are built." (Helaman 5:12.)

What, then, are we to do, if we are thus to seek him with all our hearts? I wish to suggest two preliminary qualifications, then some thoughts on the three elements of a complete testimony.

First, we must *desire* to find God above all other desires. If we want a real testimony, if we want to seek God until we find him, even if we want eternal life—all these things can be ours, if we desire them, so long as we do not desire other things more. We show what we really want by what we *do*, not just by what we *say*. So if we say we desire to grow in our faith, but the way we live suggests otherwise, we probably want something else more than we want eternal life. It might be our friends. It might be physical pleasures. Or it might only be that we don't want the Church bothering us with meetings and rules and guilt trips. Whatever it is we want so much, we are likely some day to have it. Not only will the righteous desires of our hearts be granted, the unrighteous desires of our hearts will also be granted. Over the long run, our most deeply held desires will govern our choices, one by one and day by day, until our lives finally add up to what we have really wanted.

Next, we must live worthy of having the Lord's spirit near to us. Brigham Young said:

> Pray for the Lord to inspire your hearts. Ask for wisdom and for knowledge. It is our duty to seek after it. Let us seek, and we shall find; but as for His coming down here to pour His Spirit upon you, while you are aiming after the vain and frivolous things of the world; indulging in all the vanity, nonsense, and foolery which surrounds you; drinking in all the filthy abominations which should be spurned from every community on the earth—so long as you continue this course, rest assured—he will not come near you.[3]

If we are trying to purify our desires and to live righteously, we are then in a position to build our faith in all the elements that make up a complete and deeply rooted testimony of the gospel.

I am struck by the similarity between the process of developing a testimony and the process of falling in love. Love and testimony are two of the most important human experiences, yet often we are unsure how we can be certain that either has come fully into our lives. In finding the love we seek during the courtship years, we often have in mind the personal qualities we are looking for. But even when we meet someone who has everything on our list (the test of reason), there may be something missing: the "spark," that mysterious something that makes us *feel* love, not just think it (the test of feeling). Yet rational satisfaction and good feelings are still not enough. To know if this relationship is the real thing, we must give it some time (the test of experience). We must see how things go when the "new" wears off. We need to know how the relationship holds up under pressure, whether it grows and stirs, almost whether it takes on a life of its own. As it is in the search for love, so it is in the search for testimony. Let us consider each element: reason, feeling, and experience.

The reasonableness of the gospel message speaks for itself. Indeed, religious faith is a more intellectually sound proposition than I once realized. As my experience grows in the world of reason and evidence, as well as in the world of spiritual things, I am increasingly impatient with those shallow skeptics who imply that religion must be taken solely on faith, as if no evidence for religious propositions exists — and as if no scientific propositions are taken on faith.

I agree with Alma, who told the skeptical Korihor, "All things denote there is a God; yea, even the earth, and all things that are upon the face of it, yea, and its motion." (Alma 30:44.) Scientific evidence tells us that if the earth were even slightly nearer to the sun, all life here would burn up. If it were even slightly farther away, all life here would freeze. When I read about the fiercely destructive power of earthquakes, volcanoes, and hurricanes, I see no way that we could carry on life as we do if the elements were not held in check by divine laws and powers. If we were truly at the mercy of arbitrary natural forces, wind and sand and tidal waves would bat this planet around like a leaf in a storm.

When I think about the creation, I wonder: What are the odds that a tornado spinning through a junkyard could create a DC-10?

I like the perspective of the restored gospel on the issue of "creationism" — that recently debated question of whether the public schools should be allowed to teach, as an alternative to evolution, the idea that the earth was suddenly created out of nothing. In a recent federal court case brought to test the right of a school board to introduce creationism into the public school curriculum, the judge held the attempt to be an unconstitutional establishment of religion. Part of the judge's difficulty was the absence of scientific evidence for the *ex nihilo* creation: it is inconsistent with the laws of science for matter to be created from nothing, since matter can be neither created nor destroyed, even though the elements may change their form. But, in contrast to the teachings of some other churches, the restored gospel does not teach that God created the earth from nothing. Rather, "Intelligence . . . was not created or made, neither indeed can be." Moreover, "the elements are eternal." (D&C 93:29, 33.) The earth was therefore "organized and formed" by God — but not from nothing. (See Abraham 4.)

When I think about science and religion, I recall hearing Bishop Henry B. Eyring quote the advice he and his brothers received from their father, a world famous chemist, "Remember, boys, you don't have to believe anything that isn't true."

Evidence for the claims of Joseph Smith continues to grow stronger. We needn't take his testimony and his inspired declarations only on faith — there is compelling evidence in his favor. When Joseph announced the Word of Wisdom, neither he nor anyone in the scientific community knew that tobacco causes lung cancer and is associated with many other health risks. Consider his prophecy about the Civil War. Consider his prophecy about the Latter-day Saints becoming a mighty people in the tops of the mountains of the west.

Consider his calling as a prophet while only a young man. There was nothing strange or unusual about heavenly manifestations to an inexperienced boy as part of a prophetic call. I have a friend who regards the First Vision as "so unlikely." Others speak similarly from within the prison of their twentieth century skepticism to conclude that "we just don't get books from angels"; and from such assumed premises, much incomplete reasoning flows. But if the Bible is evidence for anything, read about the callings of Noah, Abraham, Moses, Isaac, Jacob, Samuel, Isaiah, Jeremiah, Paul, and John the Revelator. *All* were called in precisely the manner that Joseph was. All spoke with God or angels, just as Joseph did.

In addition, we should consider the impressive body of recent research that authenticates many ancient practices and other factual propositions contained in the Book of Mormon on subjects ranging from the Nephite legal system to geography. (See especially the work of John W. Welch and his colleagues in the Foundation for Ancient Research and Mormon Studies at Brigham Young University.) Note, for example, the research on wordprints, which suggests that the Book of Mormon couldn't have been written by only one author. Learn also about the Hebrew poetry form called *chiasmus.* Nobody had heard of chiasmus in Joseph's day. But now this striking literary form, as clear and rigid as a limerick or a sonnet, has been discovered in ancient Hebrew literature. It has also been discovered in the Book of Mormon. Those who wrote on the golden plates knew and used Hebrew literary forms in their reformed Egyptian language—but Joseph Smith apparently didn't even know he had translated into those forms.

Then there are Thor Heyerdahl's recent expeditions in primitive reed boats across the Pacific Ocean and later the Atlantic. These trips show that small, crudely made boats could sail for thousands of miles on strong ocean currents.

Despite great efforts to do so, no one has been able to cast serious doubt on the authenticity of the Book of Mormon. So why doesn't everybody believe in its divine origins? Because God does not allow the case to become so compelling that we are forced to believe. Man's agency is too fundamental to be so compromised.

And yet, if our testimonies are based completely on empirical evidence or rational analysis, they are still more cobwebs than cable strands. Reason cannot always prevail over such opposing forces as temptation and prejudice. Also, science and history never do lead to absolute conclusions—for or against religious or other claims. Those disciplines are by their very nature subject to new evidence and new interpretations of old evidence. We would never allow in a modern court of law most of the "evidence" that passes for history in contemporary battles over the truth of this or that historical claim, because most of the available evidence violates the constitutional guarantees of due process. No one could obtain a fair trial many years after crucial events have taken place, which is one reason why laws exist to bar old legal claims.

To be strong, then, a testimony must also be built on spiritual feelings and insights. The scriptures are full of references to the influence of the Spirit on our feelings. The prophet Alma speaks of "when you feel these swelling motions," in addition to the more intellectual experience of discovering that truth can "enlighten my understanding." (Alma 32:28.) Nephi talks to his brothers about being past *feeling* and chastizes them because they could not *feel* the words of the Spirit. (See 1 Nephi 17:45.)

Moroni explains that the Holy Ghost will manifest the truth to us if we pray with a sincere heart and real intent — after doing our homework. (Moroni 10:4–5.) Nephi tells us that the Holy Ghost carries his power to the *hearts* of the children of men. (See 2 Nephi 33:1.) Thus, the men who talked with the resurrected Christ without recognizing him on the road to Emmaus said afterward, when they realized who he was, "Did not our heart burn within us, while he talked with us by the way?" (Luke 24:32.)

The Spirit can also convey a feeling of peace rather than a feeling of burning. As the Lord said to Oliver Cowdery: "Cast your mind upon the night that you cried unto me in your heart, that you might know concerning the truth of these things. Did I not speak peace to your mind concerning the matter? What greater witness can you have than from God?" (D&C 6:22–23.)

I remember the night when, as a young missionary, I first became aware of the Holy Ghost bearing witness to a sincere investigator. As my companion bore his testimony to her about the Resurrection, tears filled her eyes, and I began to feel as though my heart would burst from the overflowing of spiritual force. As we left her home, I asked my companion if he had felt anything unusual during our discussion. He smiled at me knowingly and said, "Do you know what that was?" Then, recognizing that this was a new but very important experience for me, he said,

"Elder Hafen, that was the Holy Ghost bearing witness of the truth. There is no other feeling like that. We may not feel it often. You can't turn it off and on like a water tap. But when in a rare moment it comes, you know what it is."

My companion's observation calls to mind the verse from Kahlil Gibran on love, in which I will substitute the word *Spirit* for the word *love:* "Think not that you can control the course of the Spirit, for the Spirit, if it finds you worthy, controls your course."

On a more recent occasion, I felt that same Spirit again, as did one of my children. We were gathered at one of those multifamily home evenings at the grandparents' house, with paper plates and chunks of hamburger buns and potato chips strewn all over the backyard. Little children were running and laughing with their cousins in a totally happy kind of bedlam. Then Grandpa mentioned that he would like to have everyone come into the living room and sit down. All the little grandchildren stopped playing and trooped into the house, where they sat down until they filled the living room floor. Everyone was very quiet, without knowing quite why they should be.

Grandpa stood in the center of the room, supporting himself with the back of a chair. He told us that he had been having trouble recovering from a recent surgery and felt the need for a blessing. He asked his sons-in-law to anoint him and bless him through the power of the priesthood. We surrounded his chair and performed the ordinance with great love and respect for him. As we finished, he thanked us for our faith and prayers, and he bore his testimony to his posterity. He seemed so quietly majestic, standing there talking to us. He told us that all he ever wants after he dies is to live with the very people who were in that room. Then he was done.

That was it — no song or prayer — everyone just began shuffling around to go pick up in the yard and clean up the kitchen.

Just then, one of our sons, who was about twelve, and a boy not then easily given to expressing personal feelings, came over to me. He was brushing away the tears from his eyes and asking, "Dad, what's the matter with me? Why am I crying? I'm not sad — I'm happy for Grandpa, and I just love him, and I want him to get better."

I said, "Why don't you go tell him that?" He ran to his grandpa and hugged him tightly and said something to him, then he came back to me even more visibly affected than before. He still wanted to know why he was reacting as he was. Then I told him, as my missionary companion had told me many years before, that this was the Holy Ghost. He was feeling love and appreciation for the priest-hood and was being told by the Spirit that what he sensed was true and good. Sensing that this was one of those rare teaching moments, I asked him never to forget what this felt like, because it was the witness of the Spirit.

At an earlier time in my life, I somehow gained the impression that spiritual feelings were not within the recognized categories of epistemology — the accepted ways of "knowing" things. Because inspired feelings and impressions are not necessarily empirical (based on typ-ical sensory observation) or rational (based on reasoning through logical thought processes), I mistakenly believed that they were part of some category of learning that belonged only to the Church. I have since discovered that "inner sight" is a source of knowledge that has long been recognized as legitimate and important in the intellectual heritage of Western civilization, even though various writ-ers and artists have obviously had different perspectives on the subject.

The premises from which scientists reason must come from some place, since they are not self-evident. They may begin from the findings of earlier experiments, they may be based on a hunch or a preconceived bias, they may be a purely creative hypothesis, or they may indeed be provided from a divine source. One of the most celebrated of history's explorers, Columbus, was so directed: "The spirit of God . . . came down and wrought upon the man; and he went forth upon the many waters, even unto the seed of my brethren, who were in the promised land." (1 Nephi 13:12.)

Intuitive insights have also played an important role in the arts, especially in the creative process. Nowhere is the place of divine inspiration more forthrightly acknowledged by a great artistic master than in the words of the German composer, Johannes Brahms. Brahms mentioned this very personal dimension of his experience only near the end of his long life, in an interview encouraged by his closest friend. Describing his own creative process, he said:

> I immediately feel vibrations that thrill my whole being. These are the Spirit illuminating the soul power within, and in this exalted state, I see clearly what is obscure in my ordinary moods; then I feel capable of drawing inspiration from above, as Beethoven did. . . . Straight-way the ideas flow in upon me, directly from God, and not only do I see distinct themes in my mind's eye, but they are clothed in the right forms, harmonies and orchestration.[4]

Brahms tempered this recognition of divine help with what seemed to him an obvious requirement: the need for great skill and exertion in applying the basic principles of music. I compare this to the roles of reason and experience as supplements to spiritual feelings. He said, "Don't make the mistake of thinking that because I attach such importance to inspiration from above, that that is all there is to it, by no means. Structure is just as consequential, for without craftsmanship, inspiration is as sounding brass or tinkling cymbal."[5]

Still, Brahms thought the works of "young composers who are atheists" would be "doomed to speedy oblivion, because they are utterly lacking in inspiration. Their works are purely cerebral."[6] Based on his own experience, the composer honestly believed that "the powers from which all truly great composers like Mozart, Schubert, Bach and Beethoven drew their inspiration is the same power that enabled Jesus to work his miracles. It is the power that created our earth and the whole universe."[7]

There will be both rationality and feeling in our experiences with testimony, and both are legitimate, respectable sources of knowledge. Yet we know that even spiritual feelings can be forgotten and that sometimes we may confuse lesser emotions with truly inspired impressions. Furthermore, our feelings can to some extent be influenced by unwise people who would manipulate them. And reason may not have the staying power against adversity that we will need if we are not to stand on borrowed light. Something more is necessary.

A third element in the development of testimony is simply experience. Our understanding of truth needs an incubation period, a chance to settle in and take root in preparation for the fruit that can eventually be borne. The test of time and the nurturing patience that go with it are eloquently described in Alma 32. There the thoughtful prophet teaches us what happens to the good seed after we have planted, nourished, and watered it. He warns of the hazards that are natural after the seed takes root and sprouts, when the heat of the sun can scorch the tender plant.

Alma teaches us also about the interactive relationship between faith and knowledge as part of the experiential process. After our experience confirms the early stages of growth in our testimony, it is still not an "either-or" proposition, in which we either "know" or "believe." There are elements of both. In the beginning of the process, we *cannot know* of the "surety" of God's words, for we are wholly without experience. At that stage, we act on the basis of faith, following our desires as a free will matter of choice. After our initial experiences, however, we are able to testify of what we know, for "[our] knowledge is perfect in that thing." (Alma 32:34.) Those who pay tithing when they fear they can't afford it are often blessed with new ideas to better manage their remaining funds; and suddenly they know something that nontithepayers cannot understand. From this they can generalize their witness to a knowledge, based on actual experience, that God keeps his promises. This level of certainty also becomes the foundation for the next steps in the development of "a perfect knowledge."

As our testimonies take root and draw from the rich soil of experience, we also encounter adversity. As Moroni wrote, "Dispute not because ye see not, for ye receive no witness until after the trial of your faith." (Ether 12:6.) As our knowledge grows, we learn that the wind whistles loudest around the highest peaks. It is in this stage that we learn the difference between cobwebs and cables. But

33

as we nourish our seedling testimony, building on our portion of sure knowledge by stretching the reach of our faith ever further, our confidence matures and our perspective broadens. Our learning from experience over time yields knowledge having a special kind of depth, for the maturing of our spiritual understanding reflects itself in the maturing of our own character. And one day "ye shall pluck the fruit thereof, which is most precious, which is sweet above all that is sweet, . . . and ye shall feast upon this fruit even until ye are filled." (Alma 32:42.)

With a perspective that beautifully blends both reason and feeling into the large framework of experience, Brigham Young put it this way:

> "How shall I know?" says one. By obeying the commandments given to you. The Lord has said, Go into the waters of baptism and be baptized for the remission of your sins, and you shall receive a witness that I am telling you the truth. How? By baptism and the laying on of hands alone? No. By seeing the sick healed? No, but by the Spirit that shall come unto you through obedience, which will make you feel like little children, and cause you to delight in doing good, to love your Father in Heaven and the society of the righteous. Have you malice and wrath then? No, it is taken from you, and you feel like the child in its mother's lap. You will feel kind to your children, to your brothers and sisters, to your parents and neighbors, and to all around you; you will feel a glow, as of fire, burning within you. And if you open your mouths to talk you will declare ideas which you did not formerly think of; they will flow into your mind, even such as you have not thought of for

years. The scriptures will be opened to you, and
you will see how clear and reasonable everything is which this or that Elder teaches you.
Your hearts will be comforted, you can lie down
and sleep in peace, and wake up with feelings
as pleasant as the breezes of summer. This is a
witness to you.[8]

Our testimonies draw in this way on all the dimensions
of our experience, until we look back on a lifetime of
impressions and insights that represent the complete fabric of a real testimony, woven one strong strand at a time.
When I think in that way of what it means to know the
gospel is true, many images occur to me:

Having a testimony means being alone in the mountains on a clear evening, looking at all those stars, and
sensing that your life really does have meaning; sensing
that you are not alone, that heaven is a real place and
God is a real person, and that he knows and cares about
you.

It means feeling the strength to control yourself when
the forces of evil would have you do otherwise. It's re-
alizing that this year you don't feel comfortable with those
old jokes and words your friends used to say, sensing that
you really have changed in your feelings about what matters, and now you know that you can continue to change
and become the way you want to be.

Having a testimony is being in a meeting when a man
who looks like a prophet enters the room, and feeling
your heart swell as everybody spontaneously stands up
and begins to sing, "We Thank Thee, O God, for a
Prophet," and now you want to sing too.

It's being far away from home, getting acquainted with
some decent person who doesn't know anything about

the Church, then feeling good inside as you tell him about Joseph Smith. And as you answer his questions, you say to yourself, *It's true—what I am saying is really true;* and you want your friend to understand, for his own happiness—and when he begins to see it, somehow you see it better too.

It means having something to really pray about, and after finding some quiet place where you can just talk and plead, sensing that somebody is listening to you and cares about what you are saying.

It's coming home late after a date, going to your mom's room, and telling her through your laughter or your tears how the evening was, and having her take your hand in hers to tell you that she really cares about your happiness, because she has always known you were sent to her from heaven.

Having a testimony is setting an example for a friend who mocks the Church, and after beginning to wonder if you're the one who is on the wrong track, one day hearing her say to you, "Thank you for being the way you are, for being good to me when I didn't deserve it. I know this sounds strange coming from me, but I want to live a better life. Will you help me?"

It is also kneeling over the altar in a sacred room, taking your sweetheart by the hand, half listening to the great promises being said over you by one who has authority, seeing in your mind's eye the panorama of your whole life pass before you. And you feel overcome with gratitude that you are there, for you doubt that you deserve it; yet there comes an assurance that God has accepted you now, both of you, and that love eternal and life eternal are all somehow part of the same thing.

A testimony means bouncing a little child on your

knee, and noticing for the first time that his smile is like your own; and then when you begin to feel what you know he feels, you taste what it means to have joy in your posterity.

It means seeing someone you love in temple clothes, in a casket, and hearing through your grief an inner voice assuring you with a deep peace that death is as natural as birth, and that your relationship with that person will endure. It is the peace that surpasses understanding, as your heart tells you things your mind does not know.

It is a grandmother and grandfather sitting side by side, close to the fireplace, after a day of remembering and sharing with their posterity. And as their seasoned hands touch in a moment of tender communication, slight smiles of knowing satisfaction pass between them, and they thank God once more that, despite all the tight places along the way, life's journey and the fulfillment of the Lord's promises have been sweet and good.

And though no combination of words seems complete enough to say what it all means to you, and it is almost too personal to talk about even if you could find the words, the important thing is your sense, deep down, that the gospel really is true. Then, if you continue to purify your desires and keep searching to find God, that quest will guide you and fulfill you all the days of your life.

"But if from thence thou shalt seek the Lord thy God, thou shalt find him, if thou seek him with all thy heart and with all thy soul.

"When thou art in tribulation, and all these things are come upon thee . . . , if thou turn to the Lord thy God, and shalt be obedient unto his voice, . . . he will not forsake thee." (Deuteronomy 4:29–31.)

Notes

1. *Elijah* (New York: G. Schirmer, Inc., n.d.), page 21.
2. Joseph Smith, *Lectures on Faith,* comp. N. B. Lundwall (Salt Lake City: N. B. Lundwall), 6:5, 7.
3. *Journal of Discourses,* 26 vols. (London: Latter-day Saints' Book Depot, 1854–86), 1:20.
4. Arthur M. Abell, *Talks with Great Composers* (New York: The Philosophical Library of New York, 1954), pages 5–6.
5. *Talks with Great Composers,* page 63.
6. *Talks with Great Composers,* page 21.
7. *Talks with Great Composers,* page 11.
8. *Journal of Discourses,* 3:211.

CHAPTER THREE

The Value of the Veil

Faith is not to have a perfect knowledge of things; therefore if ye have faith ye hope for things which are not seen, which are true.

(Alma 32:21.)

One of the clearest—yet at times most perplexing—themes in the history of God's dealings with mankind involves his decision to draw a veil between our world of mortality and his world of the eternities. Not only does the veil keep us from remembering our premortal past, it also keeps us from seeing many things that are presently taking place—for God, his angels, and their activities are hidden from our sight.

He has rarely parted that veil in his dealings with his children on the earth. After the Savior's resurrection, for example, he encountered two of his disciples on the road to Emmaus. They did not recognize him as he engaged them in conversation. As they told him of "Jesus of Nazareth," in whom they had "trusted" (note the past tense), it became apparent to him that they had not grasped the message of his mortal ministry. He then said, "O fools, and slow of heart to believe all that the prophets have spoken."

And then, "beginning at Moses . . . he expounded unto them in all the scriptures the things concerning himself." (See Luke 24:13–31.)

He did not tell them who he was. He taught them from the same scriptures he had used to teach them while he was in the flesh. Only later did they recognize him.

Why didn't he tell them sooner? He could have revealed the fact of his resurrection much more clearly, much more rapidly.

In another passage in Luke, we read the parable of the beggar Lazarus and the rich man who died about the same time as did Lazarus. What the rich man realized on the other side of the veil moved him to plead with father Abraham to send Lazarus back to preach repentance to the rich man's family, who remained in mortality. But Abraham replied, "They have Moses and the prophets; let them hear them.

"And he said, Nay, father Abraham: but if one went unto them from the dead, they will repent.

"And he said unto him, If they hear not Moses and the prophets, neither will they be persuaded, though one rose from the dead." (Luke 16:29–31.)

Why not?

In the first chapter of John we read about the Word, who was the life and the light of the world, a light that "shineth in darkness; and the darkness comprehended it not." (John 1:5.) Christ came into the world, but it knew him not, and his own received him not. If it is indeed eternal life to know God, why didn't the Lord reveal Christ to the people more obviously? He came so quietly.

If it is so important for us to know him today, why doesn't the Lord send a great chariot across the sky every day at noon, drawn by flying white horses? The chariot could stop right above the earth and then a voice from the great beyond could say, "And now a word from our Creator."

Why has he chosen not to do things like that?

Consider also the parable of the prodigal son. A young man came to his father and asked for his inheritance, and then, having received it, he went away and learned some important lessons from sad experience. (See Luke 15:11–32.) The father must have known what kind of trouble his boy was headed for. Wasn't there some way the father could have taught him what he was going to encounter, to help him understand what he might learn from his experience, without running the risk of losing him?

Certainly that must have occurred to our Father in the premortal existence when he considered the plan of a free experience in mortality. Caring about his children as he does, why was he willing to take the risk that many would not come back? Didn't he have the power to touch us in some miraculous way that would bypass that risk and endow all of us with the capacity to live with him in the celestial kingdom?

A verse in the book of Hebrews makes it clear that the Savior himself had to learn many of life's lessons the hard way—from experience. He "offered up prayers and supplications with strong crying and tears unto him who was able to save him from death; . . .

"Though he were a Son, yet learned he obedience by the things which he suffered;

"And being made perfect, he became the author of eternal salvation unto all them that obey him." (Hebrews 5:7–9.)

Then come those significant lines in which Paul talks about the need to give us only what we can assimilate: "Ye . . . are become such as have need of milk, and not of strong meat.

"For every one that useth milk is unskilful in the word of righteousness: for he is a babe.

"But strong meat belongeth to them that are of full age, even those who *by reason of use* have their senses *exercised* to discern both good and evil." (Hebrews 5:12–14; italics added.)

What do all of these passages have in common? Why not force people to be righteous? What is so essential about experience—so essential that it is worth the risk that we may not come back? Why is it that we who are accustomed to milk must "by reason of use" exercise our senses to become ready for meat?

Salvation is a process, as well as a goal. The process involves growth, development, and change. Thus, in mortality we must learn capacities and skills, not merely gather information. There is something about forcing people to be righteous that interferes with, even prohibits, the process that righteousness in a free environment is designed to enable. Righteous living causes something to happen to people.

There are two different kinds of knowledge. One involves such rational processes as gathering information and memorizing. The other kind of knowledge I would call skill development—learning how to play the piano or swim or take a car engine apart; learning to sing or dance or think. The process of developing toward a Christlike capacity is a matter of acquiring skills more than a matter of learning facts and figures. And there is something about the nature of developing those divine skills that makes it impossible even for God to teach us those things unless we *participate* in the process. We shouldn't expect it to be otherwise—what piano teacher could teach people to play if they were unwilling to practice? What coach could improve an athlete's skills without supervising the athlete's trials and errors during innumerable practice sessions?

Imagine an innovative music school with a revolutionary approach, in which the piano students did not have to practice. The school would teach in a purely theoretical way all the rudiments; describe in detail how to move one's fingers; go deeply into music theory and history; teach thoroughly how to read music. The students would memorize all the best books that have ever been written on how to play the piano. The course could last for four years. The students would each have a project, such as memorizing the score of a major piano concerto. They would be able to close their eyes and see the manuscript for both piano and orchestra flow through their minds—they could tell you everything about it.

Then, when the first graduate of the "Do It without Practice Piano Course" walks onto the stage of Carnegie Hall to perform his debut with the orchestra, what do you suppose will happen?

Not much. Why?

Even though "thinking" is an essential element in any form of learning, some things can be learned only by practice.

In an important book about the philosophy of knowledge, a scholar named Michael Polanyi identifies skill acquisition as a unique field of knowledge.[1] He offers the interesting insight that often the essence of a skill cannot be adequately described, measured, or specified. Hence, many skills cannot be transmitted by written descriptions and instructions intended to be memorized by later generations. In Polanyi's words:

> An art which cannot be specified in detail cannot be transmitted by prescription, since no prescription for it exists. It can be passed on only by example from master to apprentice. . . .
>
> It follows that an art which has fallen into disuse for the period of a generation is altogether lost. There are hundreds of examples of

44

this to which the process of mechanization is continuously adding new ones. These losses are usually irretrievable. It is pathetic to watch the endless efforts — equipped with microscopy and chemistry, with mathematics and electronics — to reproduce a single violin of the kind the half-literate Stradivarius turned out as a matter of routine more than two hundred years ago.[2]

Polanyi believes we can learn a skill only by imitating the skillful performance of one who has mastered the skill — even though the teacher whom we imitate cannot specify and measure every detail of his art. There is a close analogy between this idea and the central gospel concept that knowing the Savior personally and emulating his example is the ultimate way of living the gospel, a way that transcends merely following specific commandments and detailed doctrines.

Though Polanyi is not writing about religion, but about knowledge as a field of science, he does (perhaps unintentionally) make a point about religion:

> To learn by example is to submit to authority. You follow your master because you trust his manner of doing things even when you cannot analyze and account in detail for its effectiveness. By watching the master and emulating his efforts in the presence of his example, the apprentice unconsciously picks up the rules of the art, including those which are not explicitly known to the master himself. These hidden rules can be assimilated only by a person who surrenders himself to that extent uncritically to the imitation of another. A society which wants to preserve a fund of personal knowledge must submit to tradition.[3]

Most of us have known people who rejected an opportunity to test the truthfulness of the gospel because they were not willing to submit to the gospel commandments. We have pleaded with the skeptic to try the gospel and see. How impatient we have become when the skeptic wants us to prove it *first,* before he will submit himself in some way that seems to him a loss of his freedom!

If the skeptic doubts that the process of complying with gospel principles will really bear fruit, his own doubting will indeed make it impossible for the gospel to bear fruit for him. For unless he yields and participates and loses himself in it, there is no way he can find the proof he demands.

Until a person who is attempting to learn a skill is willing to commit himself totally and irrevocably, there are many things he cannot learn. Polanyi describes how a blind man with a walking stick becomes accustomed to "seeing" with it. What the stick tells him, the blind man can never fully describe to anyone else. For those who are not blind—but who merely close their eyes at times to see what it is like—are not sufficiently motivated to learn what the stick can tell them about the world. Why not? Because they don't have to know.

Unless you are blind you don't have to know.

To carry the analogy further, a blind person may say he would rather not take the risk of getting hit by a car and would prefer to just stay home. All his teacher can say is, "If you want the freedom your cane can give you, you must take that risk. I can't tell you how to learn to use the cane unless you go out there and learn by practice. I will stand by your side and talk to you, I will tell you everything I know, but if you aren't committed to it, there isn't anything I can do for you."

The blind person must somehow be persuaded that going through the agony of *practice* with the cane, a step at a time, with all the mistakes that inevitably go with practice, is worth the effort and the risks involved. The practice involved is not merely a matter of repetition; rather, it is a process of change and growth achieved by repeated mental effort aimed at learning a specific skill, in the pursuit of some purpose.

How does one convince others about things like that? Our skeptical friends may say, "What is so wonderful about the celestial kingdom? Explain it to me so I can understand it, and then maybe I can put up with all the commandments, take the risks, submit myself to the Master, and go through all the practice and routine. But first I want you to prove to me that it is all going to be worthwhile in the end."

And what can our answer be? There is no way that human minds, resurrected or not, can communicate to other human minds what it is like. We do not know why that is so. It is in the nature of reality and the nature of the universe. All we can do is trust and try it. Something will happen to those who try, and then they will know. But when they attempt to explain it to someone else, the listener likely will not understand fully what they are talking about.

Our mortal existence gives us the opportunity to develop the skills and capacities we must have to live in the celestial kingdom. When my nine-year-old boy says he wants to drive the car, I must explain to him that if he goes out onto the freeway, he is going to be dangerous — he might kill himself and a lot of other people as well. He does not yet have the *capacity* to use the freedom offered by a freeway.

Until he develops that capacity—the skill, the judgment, the maturity—driving on the freeway will kill him. The same would be true of our premature introduction to the freedom—and the responsibility—of living in a kingdom governed by celestial laws.

The assumption of responsibility can be liberating or crushing, depending upon one's preparation to receive it.

The Doctrine and Covenants teaches that "whatever principle of intelligence we attain unto in this life, it will rise with us in the resurrection." (D&C 130:18.) "Principle of intelligence" may refer to facts, information, knowledge of the commandments with all of the doctrinal variations. But it may also refer to Christlike capacity and skills— self-control, obedience, compassion, patience, unselfishness, and other virtues.

Why might we be "damned" if we saw a sign—if the veil were parted too early? We would be stopping our progress toward the development of those celestial qualities. Even if a chariot were to fly across the sky every day, seeing such wonders would not help us much to know God, and Jesus Christ whom he sent. (See John 17:3.) Since *eternal* life, which is what it means to know Christ, refers not to length of life but to *quality* of life, it involves the long-term, difficult, gradual development of the capacity to live as Christ does. When we begin to live as he does, then will we begin to know him.

Sometimes in our gospel discussions we recall the presentation of Satan's plan in the preexistence: "I will redeem all mankind, that one soul shall not be lost, and surely I will do it; wherefore give me thine honor." (Moses 4:1.) We usually say the problem with Satan's plan was that he "sought to destroy the agency of man, which I, the Lord God, had given him." (Moses 4:3.)

We might also ask why agency matters so much.

Agency is important not only in representing the abstract principle of free will. Without agency, we *cannot* develop the skills that are essential to the growth we must experience to return to God's presence. It is simply impossible. A horse can be led to water, but he cannot be forced to drink. A child can be given a book, but she will never learn to read unless she voluntarily makes an effort to read. Satan's plan *could not have worked.* His claim of guaranteeing, regardless of our choices, that not one soul would be lost was like most of his claims: it was a lie.

These ideas suggest some of the reasons why voluntary action and freedom of inquiry are essential to the development of religious character, just as they are essential to intellectual development.

The idea that salvation involves a process of skill development may also help us to understand why there is a veil. We need not be impatient that things must be the way they are—we should, rather, be grateful. These circumstances show us how faith and repentance and knowing God are processes and principles of action, understood not just by defining them but by experiencing them. God is a great teacher, and he knows the patterns and the principles we must follow in the active conduct of our lives in order to develop divine capacities. He can teach us these things—he has that power—but only if we will give ourselves to the process.

If we insist on getting a medal or a gold star on our forehead as proof that we are learning the right things, or if we insist on being able to explain to everyone else how the gospel works and why it works, even though God himself cannot explain it to our finite minds until we have developed the capacity to understand it, we will not have learned what the gospel of Jesus Christ is about. We will still be floundering around as spiritual adolescents trying to master the details of a lesser law.

The substance of our religion cannot fully be measured, it cannot fully be specified, except as it is understood by experience. But that is no reason to value it less. The most significant things we know about cannot be totally measured or specified. Our love for our families, our testimonies, our feelings of gratitude when we sense anew all that God has done for us — somehow to reduce these things to a content we can communicate entirely to other people or a meaning we can label so they will understand them fully may be to degrade their sacredness. Like beauty and joy, they are too important to be specifiable.

It should be observed, of course, that the value of learning through experience does not mean that we must make every human mistake ourselves in order to learn the lessons of life. We can learn vividly and permanently through vicarious experience, as we observe the good and bad consequences that flow from the choices other people make. There is evidence all around in today's world that "wickedness never was happiness." (Alma 41:10.)

In addition, we are not able, solely through our own effort, to develop the attributes of a Christlike perfection — even if we participate fully in the learning opportunities provided by the mortal experience. We must do all within our power, but the final achievement of celestial capacity comes ultimately through the bestowal of divine endowments. "For we know that it is by grace that we are saved, after all we can do." (2 Nephi 25:23.) "Yea, come unto Christ, and be perfected in him ... [for] by his grace ye may be perfect in Christ." (Moroni 10:32.) The Savior's atonement compensates not only for our sins but also for our inadequacies.[4] This is an important qualification on the significance of our own effort—not only because it reminds us of the mission of Christ, but because it also assures us that our own struggling is not our only resource in the quest for understanding, for meaning, and for a divine nature.

There is a veil between our world of mortality and God's world of the eternities. It can become very thin at times, but for most of us the veil remains; for he has placed it there to help us learn how we must live, what we must become, to live with him some day.

Notes

1. See *Personal Knowledge* (New York: Harper and Row, 1964).
2. *Personal Knowledge*, page 53.
3. *Personal Knowledge*, page 53.
4. See Bruce C. Hafen, *The Broken Heart* (Salt Lake City: Deseret Book, 1989.)

CHAPTER FOUR

On Dealing with Uncertainty

Behold, if it be a true seed, . . . if ye do not cast it out by your unbelief, that ye will resist the Spirit of the Lord, behold it will begin to swell within your breasts. . . . If ye will nourish the word . . . it shall take root; and . . . behold, by and by ye shall pluck the fruit thereof, which is . . . sweet above all that is sweet.

(Alma 32:28, 41–42.)

Early in life, most of us think in terms of black or white — there is very little gray in either the intellectual or the spiritual dimension of our perspective. Thus, most of the freshmen at Brigham Young University and Ricks College have a childlike optimism and loyalty that makes them wonderfully teachable and pleasant. It is typical of these young men and women to trust their teachers, to believe what they read, and to respond with boundless enthusiasm to invitations for Church service.

Where else but in a student ward comprised mostly of freshmen would you find a Church member so thrilled to be called by the bishop as hymn book coordinator, or Relief Society Sunday morning orange juice specialist? As a returned missionary told me, one thing he likes best about being in a ward of freshmen and sophomores is that when topics such as faith or repentance are raised for discussion, nobody yawns.

As time goes on, however, experience often introduces a new dimension to a student's perspective. In general, I would characterize this new dimension as a growing awareness that there is something of a gap between the real and the ideal, between what *is* and what *ought* to be.

This gap has been described elsewhere: "[I]magine

two circles, one inside the other. The inner boundary is the real, or what is. The outer boundary is the ideal, or what ought to be. We stand at the inner boundary, reaching out, trying to pull reality closer to the lofty ideals to which we have committed ourselves." We become "aware of the distance between these two boundaries when we realize that some things about ourselves are not what we wish they were, or what they ought to be. As that realization grows, so can our level of frustration."[1]

Our experience with Church-owned institutions can make us especially vulnerable to the disillusionment that sometimes follows our awareness of this gap — in part because our "ideal" expectations may be unusually high. A BYU student, for example, may find it very frustrating to do battle with the great red tape machines that seem to control the processes of admission, registering for classes, or transferring credits from another college. She may remain unknown and nameless to her student ward bishop for weeks or even months, or she may brush up against a faculty member whose Church commitments are less visible than she had expected them to be.

At a more personal, and therefore more spiritual, level, perhaps an important prayer goes too long unanswered; or one suffers a devastating setback with grades, with good health, or with the prospects for marriage. And in such times of great need, the heavens may seem closed. One may also become increasingly conscious of others' imperfections, including those of parents, other Church members, or a Church leader. When we become acquainted at an adult level with those who have been our heroes, we naturally begin to see their human limitations. LDS students may also find themselves struggling to clarify the previously unarticulated assumptions of their personal worldview, as they first confront such controversial topics as feminism or differing political views among Church members.

New missionaries may discover a jarring sense of distance between the real and the ideal as they move from the "pre-existence" of the Missionary Training Center to the "mortality" of daily life in an assigned field of labor. I vividly recall my feelings of overwhelming discouragement during my first few weeks as a missionary in a foreign country. I had studied the language in college, but hearing the "natives" speak their mother tongue initially sounded in my ears as so much gibberish; I understood virtually nothing and was literally speechless for the first time I could remember.

And even after the language began to make sense, I repeatedly fought back the tears of disappointment when, in other dimensions of missionary service, the promised fruits of a "positive mental attitude" seemed frequently to elude me. I recall, for instance, my combined feeling of disbelief and pain the night we dropped off a newly baptized couple in front of their apartment, then after turning around down the block and driving past their apartment going the other way, our headlights illuminated the image of the new convert—his hair still wet from the baptism—lighting up a cigarette just outside his front door.

There is a kind of poignancy in those moments when we first discover that there might be some limitations to the idea that you can do anything you make up your mind to do. I once gave everything I had to that proposition, in my determination to be the greatest shot-putter in the history of my junior high school. But I simply was not big enough—it really was hopeless.

Experiences such as these can produce confusion and uncertainty—in a word, ambiguity—and we may yearn with nostalgia for simpler, easier times, when life seemed not only more clear but more under our control. We might sense within ourselves the beginnings of skepticism, of criticism, of unwillingness to respond to authority or to invitations to commit ourselves to high-sounding goals or projects that are not very realistic.

Not everybody will encounter what I have been describing, and I do not mean to suggest that everyone *must* encounter such experiences. However, college students are probably more likely to encounter "ambiguity" than almost any other group.

The fundamental teachings of the restored gospel are potent, clear, and unambiguous. However, it is possible on occasion to encounter some ambiguity even in studying the scriptures. Consider, for example, the case of Nephi, who killed Laban in order to obtain the brass plates of scripture. That situation is not free from ambiguity until the reader realizes that God himself, who gave the original commandment against murder, was also the origin of Nephi's instructions in that exceptional case.

Consider also the case of Peter on the night he denied any knowledge of his Master three times in succession. We typically regard Peter as something of a weakling whose commitment was not strong enough to make him rise to the Savior's defense. But I once heard President Spencer W. Kimball offer an alternative interpretation of Peter's behavior. In a talk to a BYU audience in 1971, President Kimball, then a member of the Council of the Twelve, said the Savior's statement that Peter would deny him three times before the cock crowed just might have been a request to Peter, not a prediction. Jesus might have been instructing his chief Apostle to deny any association with him in order to ensure strong leadership for the Church after the Crucifixion.[2]

As President Kimball asked in his talk, who could doubt Peter's willingness to stand up and be counted? Think of his boldness in striking off the guard's ear with his sword when the Savior was arrested in Gethsemane. President Kimball did not offer this view as the only interpretation, but he did suggest there is enough justification for it that it should be considered. So what is the answer— was Peter a coward, or was he so crucial to the survival of the Church that he was prohibited from risking his life? We are not sure. The scriptures don't give us enough information about Peter's motivation to clarify the ambiguity.

Consider other passages. The Lord has said that he cannot look upon sin with the least degree of allowance. (See D&C 1:31.) Yet elsewhere he said, "I have forgiven you your sins." (D&C 64:3.) There is indeed a principle of justice, but there is also a principle of mercy. At times these two correct principles can seem inconsistent, until the unifying higher principle of the Atonement does its work.

Moreover, the Savior said, "Do not your alms before men, to be seen of them." (Matthew 6:1.) But he also said, "Let your light so shine before men, that they may see your good works." (Matthew 5:16.)

Finally, he once said, "In me ye might have peace." (John 16:33.) And the angels, in announcing his coming, sang, "On earth peace, good will toward men." (Luke 2:14.) "For unto us a child is born . . . The Prince of Peace." (Isaiah 9:6.) Yet elsewhere he said, "Think not that I am come to send peace on earth: I came not to send peace, but a sword." (Matthew 10:34.)

These references illustrate that even though God has given us correct principles by which we may govern ourselves, these very principles may at times be in conflict. Choosing between two principled alternatives (two "goods") is far more difficult than choosing when a stark and obvious contrast pits good against evil.

We face concrete examples of that process every day as we attempt to fulfill our duties to family, church, community, and professional concerns. I remember hearing a young mother of several children, who had a responsible Church position and a busy husband, express her bewilderment as she tried to decide what should come first in her life and when. Someone advised her, "Well, just be sure you put the Lord's work first." Her reply was, "But what if it is *all* the Lord's work?"

My wife and I often wonder how we should deal with our children in circumstances that were not anticipated by any of the books on child-rearing. Sometimes one of us has a clear feeling about what should be done, but often I have no idea what approach is best, so I simply defer to her with great conviction, "Well, dear, just be sure you do the right thing."

Church and family life are not the only places where the right answer is not always on the tip of our tongues. If you would stretch your mind about the implications of ambiguity, think back to the Viet Nam War—should our nation have tried to do more or less than it did? Or consider whether we should sell all we have and donate our surplus to the millions of people who are starving. We might also ask how much governmental intervention into the regulation of business and private life is too much.

The people on the extreme sides of these questions convey great certainty about what should be done. However, I think some of these people would rather be certain than right.

Turning to one more fertile field to illustrate the naturalness of ambiguity, I remember Arthur Henry King's statement that most truly great literary works raise a profound question about a human problem, explore the question skillfully and in depth, and then leave the matter for the reader to resolve. He added that if the resolution seems too clear or too easy, the literature is perhaps not very good, or else those reading it have missed its point.

Recall, for example, Dostoevsky's novel, *The Idiot,* where the question is seriously raised whether it is possible for a true Christian to love unselfishly. The main character in the story is a pure and good man who loves two different women in two very different ways. One he loves as most men love women — she cares for him, she helps him, he is attracted to her romantically, and she could make his life very happy. The other woman — a pathetically inadequate person — he loves primarily because she needs him desperately and he has a compassionate heart. Posing the dilemma of which woman the man should marry, Dostoesvky seems to ask whether it is realistically possible to be totally devoted to the unselfish ideals of Christianity. As we might expect, he leaves that huge question unresolved, forcing the reader to ponder it for himself.

I have intentionally tried to suggest a wide variety of instances in which the answers we may seek are not as obvious as we might have expected. My suggestion is that some uncertainty is characteristic of the mortal experience. The mists of darkness in Lehi's dream are, for that very reason, a strong symbolic representation of life as we face it on this planet. There are, of course, many things very certain and very clear, as so beautifully represented by the iron rod in Lehi's dream; but there is enough complexity to make the topic of ambiguity worthy of discussion.

Given, then, the existence of a gap for most of us between where we stand and where we would like to be, and given that we will have at least some experiences that make us wonder what we are to do, I think there are three different levels in dealing with ambiguity.

At level one, there are two typical attitudes, one of which is that we simply do not — perhaps cannot — even see the problems that exist. Some seem almost consciously to filter out any perception of a gap between the real and the ideal. For those in this category, the gospel at its best is a firm handshake, an enthusiastic greeting, and a smiley button. Their mission was the best, their ward is the best, and every new day is probably going to be the best day they ever had. These cheerful ones are happy, spontaneous, optimistic, and they always manage to hang loose. They are able to weather many storms that would seem formidable to more pessimistic types, though one wonders if they have somehow missed hearing that a storm was going on.

A second group at level one has quite a different problem with the gap between what is and what ought to be. Those in this category eliminate the frustrating distance between the real and the ideal by, in effect, erasing the inner circle of reality. They cling to the ideal so single-mindedly that they just don't feel the pain that would come from facing the truth about themselves, about others, or about the world around them. I suppose it is this category that is so frequently represented in the letters to the editor of the school papers at BYU and Ricks, where such shock is occasionally expressed that some person or some part of the institution has fallen short of perfection and the writer is aghast — "surely not at the Lord's university."

Those in this group seem unable to distinguish between imperfections that matter a great deal and those that may not matter so much. I think Hugh Nibley must have had them in mind when he once spoke of those who find it more commendable to get up at 5:00 A.M. to write a bad book than it is to get up at 9:00 A.M. to write a good book. While self-discipline is a virtue, it is obvious to Brother Nibley that the exact hour when we arise is not as important as what we do once we are up.

I recall a group of students who once discussed which of the two types of people I have just described offered the most appropriate model for emulation. They felt they had to choose between being relaxed and happy about the gospel or being an intense perfectionist. After listening to the discussion, I felt that both of these categories suffer from the same limitation. It is not much of a choice when one must select between a frantic concern with perfection and a forced superficial happiness.

Both perspectives lack depth; they understand things too quickly, and they may draw conclusions from their experience too easily. Neither is well prepared for adversity, and I fear that the first strong wind that comes along will blow them over. I believe this is primarily because their roots have not sunk far enough into the soil of experience to establish a firm foundation. Both also reflect the thinness of a philosophy that is untempered by common sense. In both cases, it would be helpful simply to be more realistic about life's experiences, even if that means facing some questions and limitations that leave us feeling uncomfortable. That very discomfort can motivate us toward real growth. As President Harold B. Lee said, the true church is intended not only to comfort the afflicted, but to afflict the comfortable.

We should then step up to level two, where we see things for what they are, for only then can we deal with reality in a meaningful and constructive way.

If we are not willing to grapple with the frustration that comes from facing bravely the uncertainties we encounter, we may never develop the kind of spiritual maturity that is necessary for our ultimate preparations. Heber C. Kimball once said the Church has yet to pass through some very close places, and those who are living on "borrowed light" will not be able to stand when those days come.

We need to develop the capacity to form judgments of our own about the value of ideas, opportunities, or people who may come into our lives. We won't always have the security of knowing whether a certain idea is "Church approved," because new ideas don't always come along with little tags attached to them saying whether they have been reviewed at Church headquarters. Whether in the form of music, books, friends, or opportunities to serve, there is much that is lovely, of good report, and praiseworthy that is not the subject of detailed discussion in Church manuals or courses of instruction. Those who will not risk exposure to experiences that are not obviously related to some Church word or program will, I believe, live less abundant and meaningful lives than the Lord intends.

We must develop sufficient independence of judgment

and maturity of perspective that we are prepared to handle the shafts and whirlwinds of adversity and contradiction that may come to us. When those times come, we cannot be living on borrowed light. We should not be deceived by the clear-cut labels others may use to describe circumstances that are, in fact, not so clear. Our encounters with reality and disappointment are, actually, vital stages in the development of our maturity and understanding.

Despite the value of a level-two awareness, however, there are some serious hazards at this stage. One's acceptance of the clouds of uncertainty may be so complete that the iron rod fades into the receding mist and skepticism becomes a guiding philosophy. Often, this perspective comes from erasing the *outer* circle, representing the ideal, or what ought to be, and then focusing excessively on the inner circle of reality.

While teaching law school, I noticed how common it is for first-year law students to experience great frustration as they discover that our legal system is characterized not by hard, fast rules, but by legal principles that often appear to contradict each other. I recall one new student who approached me after class to express the confusion he was encountering in his study of the law. He said he had what he called "a low tolerance for ambiguity." He had been wondering if part of his problem was that only weeks before, he had returned from a mission, where everything was crisp and clear, where even many of the words he spoke were provided for him. To feel successful, all he had to do was follow the step-by-step plan given him for each day and each task on his mission. Law school was making him feel totally at sea as he groped for simple guidelines that would tell him what to do. His circumstance was one more example of what is typical of college and university students in the early years of their experience.

However, by the time our law students reach their third year of study, it is not uncommon for them to develop such a *high* tolerance for ambiguity that they are skeptical about everything. Where formerly they felt they had all the answers, but just did not know what the questions were, they now seem to have all the questions but few of the answers.

I find myself wanting to tell our third-year law students that those who take too much delight in their finely honed tools of skepticism and dispassionate analysis will limit their effectiveness, in the Church and elsewhere, because they can become contentious, standoffish, arrogant, and unwilling to commit themselves. I have seen some of them try out their new intellectual tools in a priesthood quorum or a Sunday School class. A well-meaning teacher will make a point they think is a little silly, and they will feel an irresistible urge to leap to their feet and publicly deflate the teacher's momentum. If they are successful, they begin looking for other opportunities to point out the exception to any rule anybody can state. They begin to delight in cross-examination of the unsuspecting, just looking for somebody's bubble of idealism floating around so that they can pop it with their shiny new pin of skepticism. And in all that, they fail to realize that when some of those bubbles pop, out goes much of the feeling of trust, loyalty, harmony, and sincerity so essential to preserving the Spirit of the Lord.

If that begins to happen in *our* wards, in *our* homes, or in *our* marriages, we will have begun to destroy the fragile fabric of trust that binds us together in all loving relationships. People may come away from their encounters with us wondering how we can possibly have a deep commitment to the gospel and say some of the things we say.

I am not suggesting that we should always just smile and nod our approval, implying that everything is wonderful and that our highest hope is for everybody to have a nice day. That is level one. I *am* suggesting that we must realize the potential for evil as well as good that may come with what education can do to our minds and our way of dealing with other people.

The dangers of which I speak are not limited to our relations with others. They can become very personal, prying into our own hearts in unhealthy ways. The ability to acknowledge ambiguity is not a final form of enlightenment. Once our increased tolerance and patience enable us to look longer and harder at difficult questions and pat answers, we must be very careful, lest our basic posture toward Church-related matters gradually shift from being committed to being noncommittal. That is not a healthy posture.

Indeed, in many ways, a Church member who moves from a stage of commitment to a stage of being tentative and noncommittal is in a worse position than one who has never experienced a basic commitment. The previously committed person may too easily assume that he has already been through the "positive-mental-attitude" routine and "knows better" now, as he judges things. He may assume that being submissive, meek, obedient, and humble are matters with which he is already familiar, and that he has finally outgrown the need to work very hard at being that way again. Those are the assumptions of a hardened heart.

I once had an experience that taught me a great lesson about the way a highly developed tolerance for "being realistic" can inhibit the workings of the Spirit in our lives. When I had been on my mission in Germany about a year, I was assigned to work with a brand new missionary named Elder Keeler, who had just arrived fresh from converting, so he thought, all the stewardesses on the plane from New York to Frankfurt. Within a few days of his arrival, I was called to a meeting in another city and had to leave him to work in our city with another inexperienced missionary whose companion went with me. I returned late that night.

The next morning I asked him how his day had gone. He broke into an enthusiastic smile and said he had found a family who would surely join the Church. In our mission, it was rare to see anyone join the Church, let alone a whole family. I asked for more details, but in his excitement he had forgotten to write down either the name or the address. All he could remember was that the family lived on the top floor of a big apartment house. "Oh, that's great," I thought to myself as I contemplated all those flights of stairs. He also explained that he knew so little German that he had exchanged but a few words with the woman who answered the door. But he did think she wanted us to come back — and he wanted to go find her and have me talk to her that very minute. I explained that the people who don't slam the door in our faces do not necessarily intend to join the Church. But off we went to find her, mostly to humor him. He couldn't remember the right street, either, so we picked a likely spot and began climbing up and down those endless polished staircases.

After a frustrating hour, I decided I had to level with

him. Based on my many months of experience, I said, it was simply not worth our time to try any longer to find her. I had developed a tolerance for the realities of missionary work and simply knew more than he did about it. His eyes filled with tears and his lower lip began to tremble. "Elder Hafen," he said, "I came on my mission to find the honest in heart. The Spirit *told* me that that woman will someday be a member of the Church." So I decided to teach him a lesson. I raced him up one staircase after another until he was ready to drop, and so was I. "Elder Keeler," I asked, "had enough?" "No," he said. "We've got to find her." I began to smolder. I decided to work him until he begged to stop — then maybe he would get the message.

Finally at the top of a long flight of stairs, we found the apartment. She came to the door. He thrashed my ribs with his elbow, and whispered loudly, "That's her, Elder. That's the one. Talk to her!"

Not long ago, that woman, her husband, and two of their five children were in our home. They had come from Germany to pick up their son, who had just completed a mission in northern Utah. Their oldest daughter has served a mission in northern Germany, the woman has been a Relief Society president, and her husband has been a bishop. We enjoyed a long, refreshing visit with them, recalling our memories of their conversion experience and sharing our experiences in the Church over the course of twenty years.

That experience is a lesson I can never forget about the limitations of skepticism and the tolerance for ambiguity that comes with learning and experience. I hope that I will never be so aware of "reality" that I am unresponsive to the whisperings of heaven.

It seems to me that the most productive response to ambiguity is at level three, where we view things not only with our eyes wide open but with our hearts wide open as well. When we do that, there will be many times when we are called upon to take some action, even though we need more evidence before knowing what to do. Such occasions may range from following the counsel of the prophets when we don't understand the basis for their conclusions, to accepting a home-teaching assignment when we are far too busy to take on any more projects. My experience has taught me always to give the Lord and his Church the benefit of any doubts I may have when some such case seems too close to call.

I stress that the willingness to be believing and accepting in these cases is a very different matter from blind obedience. It is, rather, a loving and knowing kind of obedience.

The English writer G. K. Chesterton once distinguished among "optimists," "pessimists," and "improvers," which roughly corresponds to my three levels of dealing with ambiguity. He concluded that both the optimists and the pessimists look too much at only one side of things. He observed that neither the extreme optimist nor the extreme pessimist would ever be of much help in *improving* the human condition, because people can't solve problems unless they are willing to acknowledge that a problem exists and yet also retain enough genuine loyalty to do something about it.

More specifically, Chesterton wrote that the evil of the excessive optimist (level one) is that he will "defend the indefensible. He is the jingo of the universe; he will say, 'My cosmos, right or wrong.' He will be less inclined to the reform of things; more inclined to a sort of frontbench official answer to all attacks, soothing everyone with assurances. He will not wash the world, but white-wash the world."

On the other hand, the evil of the pessimist (level two), wrote Chesterton, is "not that he chastises gods and men, but that he does not love what he chastises." In being the so-called "candid friend," the pessimist is not really candid. Chesterton continued: "He is keeping some-thing back—his own gloomy pleasure in saying unpleas-ant things. He has a secret desire to hurt, not merely to help. . . . He is using the ugly knowledge which was al-lowed him [in order] to strengthen the army, to discourage people from joining it."[3]

In going on to describe the "improvers," or level three, Chesterton illustrates by referring to women who are loyal to those who need them:

> Some stupid people started the idea that be-cause women obviously back up their own people through everything, therefore women are blind and do not see anything. They can hardly have known any women. The same women who are ready to defend their men through thick and thin . . . are almost morbidly lucid about the thinness of his excuses or the thickness of his head. . . . Love is not blind; that is the last thing that it is. Love is bound; and the more it is bound the less it is blind.[4]

Perhaps President Harold B. Lee was thinking of Ches-terton's point about women when he used to say, "Behind every great man, there is an amazed woman."

Chesterton's arranging of these categories makes me think of one other way to compare the differing levels of perspective that people bring to the way they cope with ambiguity. Consider the metaphorical image of "lead, kindly light." At level one, people either do not or cannot see that there are *both* a kindly light and an encircling gloom, or even if they see both, they can discern no real difference between the two. At level two, the difference is acutely apparent, but one's acceptance of the ambiguity may be so wholeheartedly pessimistic as to say, "Remember that the hour is darkest just before everything goes completely black."

How different are these responses from that calm but honest prayer at level three,

> *Lead, kindly Light,*
> *Amid th'encircling gloom;*
> *Lead thou me on. . . .*
> *I do not ask to see*
> *The distant scene —*
> *One step enough for me.*[5]

Consider now a final illustration of one who stood at level three. He had passed from level one because his eyes were fully open to the reality, including some of the pain, of seeing things for what they were. Yet he had moved from a level-two kind of realism to a third level where his mature perspective permitted what he saw with those wide-open eyes to be subordinated to what he felt in a wide-open heart.

The man in this case was my own father, who died some years ago. At the time of this incident, he was in his mid-fifties and was very involved in his professional life and in other heavy obligations that frequently took him out of town for several days at a time. He was tired. At a much earlier time in his life he had served for ten years in a stake presidency and had fulfilled numerous other assignments for the Church. One day a friend approached him saying that he had just been called to be the bishop of their ward. He felt he couldn't possibly accept the assignment unless my father would act as his first counselor.

It is one thing to be called as a counselor in the bishopric when one is young and full of fresh enthusiasm to learn about leadership in the Church, and when one's time is not heavily committed. One might understandably have a somewhat different attitude at a later time in life. Here are the inner thoughts of my father's heart as he wrote them that day in his personal journal:

> My first reaction was, if it be possible, let this cup pass from me. . . . I know something of the work required of a bishopric; it is a constant, continual grind; there is no let up. . . . I am busy and my state affairs demand what spare time and energy I have. In some respects I am not humble and prayerful enough; I have not always been willing to submit unquestioningly to all the decisions of the Church . . . but neither do I feel that I can say no to any call that is made by the Church, and so now I add to my first reaction, "Nevertheless, not as I will, but as Thou wilt."
>
> I will resolve to do it as best I can. There will be times when I will chafe under the endless meetings, but I am going to get in tune with the program of the Church in every way. I do not intend to get sanctimonious, but I know there must be no reservations in my heart about my duties and responsibilities. The work of the Church will have to come first. It will not be hard for me to pay my tithing and attend regularly, as I have been doing that. But I will have

to learn, I suppose, to love the *Deseret News,* or at least the Church Section, as much as I love the *Tribune. . . .* I will have to get to the temple more often. . . . I will have to become better acquainted with the ward members and be genuinely interested in them and their problems. . . . I will have to learn to love every one of them and to dispose myself in such a way that they might find it possible to feel the same toward me. Perhaps in my weak way I will have to try and live as close to the Lord as we expect the General Authorities to do.

Perhaps my appreciation for understatement and my personal knowledge that my father was an honest man make that statement seem to me a more striking example of dealing humbly with ambiguity than it really is. But his statement stirs me to want to be as childlike as my education has taught me to be tough-minded—to be wise as a serpent and harmless as a dove, as the Savior said.

I hope we may be honest and courageous enough to face squarely the uncertainties we encounter, try to understand them, and then do something about them. Perhaps then we will not be living on borrowed light. "Love is not blind; that is the last thing that it is. Love is bound; and the more it is bound the less it is blind."

Notes

1. *The Broken Heart,* page 177.
2. "Peter, My Brother," *BYU Devotional Speeches of the Year,* 13 July 1971.
3. Gilbert K. Chesterton, *Orthodoxy* (Garden City, New York: Images Book, 1959), pages 69–70.
4. *Orthodoxy,* page 71.
5. *Hymns of The Church of Jesus Christ of Latter-day Saints* (Salt Lake City: The Church of Jesus Christ of Latter-day Saints, 1985), no. 97.

CHAPTER FIVE

"Their Arm Shall Be My Arm"

But if ye neglect the tree, and take no thought for its nourishment, behold it will not get any root; . . . Now, this is not because the seed was not good, neither is it because the fruit thereof would not be desirable; but it is because . . . ye will not nourish the tree, therefore ye cannot have the fruit thereof.
(Alma 32:38–39.)

T he American writer and teacher William James explored the need for a believing heart a century ago in two memorable talks to college students: "The Will to Believe" and "Is Life Worth Living?" James said, "The question of having moral beliefs . . . is decided by our *will.* . . . If your heart does not *want* a world of moral reality, your head will assuredly never make you believe in one."[1]

James also suggested the stirring idea that our freely chosen willingness to believe may actually be a determining factor in whether God's promises to us can be fulfilled — in part because our beliefs impel the actions that *only we* can take to "nourish" the seed of faith in its growth toward becoming the tree of eternal life. Even though it is God's greatest work and his glory to see us enjoy eternal life (see Moses 1:39), if we "neglect the tree [of eternal life], and take no thought for its nourishment" (Alma 32:38), no matter how good the seed nor how sweet the fruit, "ye *cannot* have the fruit thereof" (Alma 32:39). If we deny ourselves that blessing, not only are we left unfulfilled, but we also frustrate God's own desires to bless his children. Using James' phrase, "God himself . . . may draw vital strength and increase of very being from our fidelity."[2]

Prompted by this idea, this chapter will consider the

possibility that our spiritual development not only depends on the Lord's help, but that *he* depends on *our* help to enable that development. Our context for developing this thought will be the ongoing struggle between good and evil.

As a backdrop for that discussion, we should place William James' idea into its natural environment in his thoughts about the attitude of being believing. One of his best-known insights regarding "the will to believe" is that the agnostic attitude (the stance of delaying a decision on questions of religious faith until more tangible evidence exists) is simply impossible as a practical matter. Indeed, agnosticism can lead to the same outcome as deliberate atheism:

> [B]elief and doubt are living attitudes, and involve conduct on our part. . . . If I doubt that you are worthy of my confidence, I keep you uninformed of all my secrets just as if you were *un*worthy of the same. If I doubt the need of insuring my house, I leave it uninsured as much as if I believed there were no need. . . . There are . . . inevitable occasions in life when inaction . . . must count as action, and when not to be *for* is to be practically *against;* and in all such cases strict and consistent neutrality is an unattainable thing.[3]

Thus, because our own attitudes and choices heavily influence the outcomes of our life experience, James believes that whether life is worth living "depends on the liver" — that is, on who is living it. This is because "optimism and pessimism are definitions of the world," and our own reactions to the world necessarily determine which definition is correct. Because the way life treats us depends so much on how we treat life, we are constantly at risk:

"Not a victory is gained, not a deed of faithfulness or courage is done, except upon a *maybe;* not a service, . . . not a scientific exploration or experiment or textbook, that may not be a mistake. It is only by risking our persons from one hour to another that we live at all. And *often enough our faith beforehand in an uncertified result is the only thing that makes the result come true.*"[4]

James asks us to suppose that we are climbing a mountain, and we have worked ourselves into a position from which the only escape is by leaping across a deep chasm. Of this predicament he writes, "Have faith that you can successfully make" the terrible leap, "and your feet are nerved to its accomplishment. But mistrust yourself . . . and you will hesitate so long that, at last, all unstrung and trembling . . . you roll in the abyss. . . . Refuse to believe, and you shall indeed be right, for you shall irretrievably perish. But believe, and again you shall be right, for you shall save yourself. You make one or the other of two possible universes true by your trust or mistrust—both universes having been only *maybes,* in this particular, before you contributed your act."[5]

In this way, our faith in the unseen world inspires us to do the things that allow the fruits of God's promises to be demonstrated in the visible world. Unless we freely choose to be involved, some of God's promises will remain as unfulfilled as if they did not exist. For example, unless we repent, we are as lost as if there were no Atonement: "[H]e that . . . goes on in the ways of sin . . . remaineth in his fallen state. . . . Therefore, he is as though there was no redemption made." (Mosiah 16:5.) This validation process leads James to the central point of this chapter:

I confess that I do not see why the very [mean-
ing] of [the] invisible world may not in part
depend on the personal response which any
one of us may make to the religious appeal.
*God himself, in short, may draw vital strength
and increase of very being from our fidelity.*
For my own part, I do not know what the sweat
and blood and tragedy of this life mean, if they
mean anything short of this. If this life be not
a real fight, in which something is eternally
gained for the universe by success, it is no better
than a game of private theatricals from which
one may withdraw at will. But it *feels* like a real
fight — as if there were something really wild in
the universe which *we* are needed to redeem;
and first of all to redeem our own hearts from
atheisms and fears. For such a half-wild, half-
saved universe our nature is adapted. The deep-
est thing in our nature is this . . . dumb religion
of the heart in which we dwell alone with our
willingnesses and unwillingnesses, our faiths
and fears.[6]

Is it possible that God himself "may draw vital strength
and increase of very being from our fidelity"? I believe
it is possible, not only because we must nourish the seed
of faith in our own lives, but also because he needs us
to help nourish those seeds in the lives of others.

One helpful framework for developing the idea that
God needs our help is to consider the conflict between
Good and Evil — a very real war in which we are all par-
ticipants. Our part in that war is intensely personal when
the forces of Good and Evil pull us in opposing directions.
Our part is also a critical element in assisting *others* to
cope with evil forces, which in turn helps the "Lord of

our far-flung battle line" win his own victories in the war for his children's souls.[7] He has already summoned us to this duty and sent forth the battle cry: "[L]et my army become very great, and let it be sanctified before me." (D&C 105:31.)

Recent historical developments have taken a turn that can sharpen our perspective on the current state of this Great War. During the late 1980s and early 1990s, we have seen, read, and almost literally felt the world tipping over the steep edge of an historical watershed in Eastern Europe and in the Soviet Union. The events of this period have rearranged our basic assumptions about the future course of world history. For nearly half a century, we were unable to imagine the world on any terms other than a continuing struggle between the free and the communist worlds. Of course, communism is far from finished in China, Russia, or other places; but the power of communist ideology as a dominant worldwide force seems mortally wounded.

That notion—the apparently impending collapse of communist idealogy—led political theorist Francis Fukuyama to ask whether we are approaching "the end of history."[8] Fukuyama's question was based on German philosopher Georg Hegel's theory that the natural pendulum of human history swings events and cultures through an inevitable spiraling process that is beyond our power to control. Karl Marx's entire theory of communism drew upon Hegel's vision of history, including Marx's prediction that the long-term economic tensions of "dialectical materialism" would lead to the ultimate collapse of capitalism. This vision has had such power in the communist world that it seemed to dictate not only the events of history, but it also dictated everyday political policy and prescribed the place of each individual as a tiny pawn controlled by a vast, universal system.

Recent events have shattered the legitimacy of Marxist theory, which also seems to shatter the assumption that the world might be moving toward some large-scale historical end. As the world rubs its eyes in disbelief at the rubble of this disintegrating theory of history, Fukuyama suggests that the ideology of the liberal-democratic states, whose philosophical roots are located in the French and American revolutions, is the only game in town. Future historical events will of course continue, but on a random and unpredictable basis rather than toward the development of some grand design.

It is both a strength and a weakness that democratic liberalism makes no claim to a grand Hegelian plan of history. Democratic theory puts its entire trust in the voice of the people, a voice that does not sing to a predetermined script. This fact about democracy is its greatest blessing, but it is also its Achilles heel. As King Mosiah wisely foresaw: "Now it is not common that the voice of the people desireth anything contrary to that which is right; . . . [But] *if the time comes that the voice of the people doth choose iniquity, then is the time that the judgments of God will come upon you.*" (Mosiah 29:26–27; emphasis added.)

Once the spectre of communism is removed from our vision, we can actually see the real struggle of human history more clearly. That struggle is, as it has always been, both an ideological and a personal contest not between competing economic or political theories, but between Good and Evil. The future does not hinge on whether Karl Marx or Thomas Jefferson correctly predicted which fates control our destiny, but on whether the people "doth choose iniquity." Emerging political freedoms will increasingly free people to choose or reject moral beliefs. But if their hearts do not *want* a world of moral reality, neither their governments nor their heads will make them believe in one.

Are we at the end of cosmic-level developments in history? Not quite. The Iron Curtain is rising, but only on the next act in a greater drama, a mightier war, that must yet be played out. There will be a real end of history, but not yet.

Over the past few years, even as Zion has begun enlarging her borders and stretching her stakes across the globe, the Evil One has also been lengthening *his* stride, moving over the landscape like Darth Vader in seven-league boots. We can feel the earth shake as he moves, because, as C.S. Lewis wrote, this world is "enemy-occupied territory," for "an evil power has made himself for the present the Prince of this World." Lewis continued: "Christianity is the story of how the rightful king has landed, you might say landed in disguise, and is calling us all to take part in a great campaign....When you go to church you are really listening in on the secret wireless from our [allies]; that is why the enemy is so anxious to prevent us from going."[9]

The momentum of this war currently favors the enemy who occupies the territory. A few years ago, the Russian writer Aleksandr Solzhenitsyn delivered a disturbing commencement address at Harvard University in which he lamented the choices the free world has been making. Thundering like an Old Testament prophet, Solzhenitsyn decried the irony he sees in America's having *voluntarily* embraced the same atheistic materialism that communism forced on his beloved Russia. He believes the Western democracies have destroyed the concept of the "Supreme Complete Entity which used to restrain our passions and our irresponsibility." We have deprived ourselves of "our most precious possession: our spiritual life. *It is trampled by the party mob in the East, by the commercial one in the West.*"[10]

We may indeed be approaching a kind of final showdown in the war of all the ages; and that will be the real end of history. As the modern prophets have noted in public statements over the past few years,[11] we are now living in the time prophesied through Joseph Smith, "when peace shall be taken from the earth, and the devil shall have power over his own dominion." (D&C 1:35.) Yet, as was also prophesied for this same historical moment, "The Lord shall have power over his saints, and shall reign in their midst." (D&C 1:36.)

In these days, the pace and intensity of the great war have quickened, as the spiritual equivalent of atomic weapons and globally effective laser guns has taken the place of the arrows, muskets, and tanks of earlier regional struggles. This, then, is a time when the Lord needs not just any instruments in his hands, but finely honed ones — instruments prepared to sustain a climate of freedom and be a light unto the world until the final work is done.

In these times the Lord just might need us very much. He especially needs able, gifted men and women whose entire foundation for life is a commitment of sacrifice and uncompromising faithfulness toward building his kingdom and establishing Zion.

Sidney Rigdon was a talented man whom the Lord invited to lend his talents to the cause of Zion. Tragically, Sidney Rigdon's life did not ultimately rise to that opportunity. But the Lord's words to Sidney in 1830 might also have been addressed to the modern Saints whose gifts and talents are needed in these days of intensifying conflict:

> And the time speedily cometh that great things are to be shown forth unto the children of men; But without faith shall not anything be shown forth except desolations upon Babylon. . . . Wherefore, I call upon the weak things of the world, those who are unlearned and despised, to thrash the nations by the power of my Spirit; And *their arm shall be my arm*, and I will be their shield and their buckler; and I will gird up their loins, and they shall fight manfully for me; . . . Keep all the commandments . . . and I will cause the heavens to shake for your good, and Satan shall tremble and Zion shall rejoice upon the hills and flourish. . . . Fear not, little flock, the kingdom is yours until I come. Behold, I come quickly. (D&C 35:10–11, 13–14, 24, 27; emphasis added.)

Unless we live in such a way that our natural talents are enhanced "by the power of [his] spirit," we are not of much use to the Lord's cause, no matter how gifted we may seem. But if we do live worthy of divine help, even those who may seem weak and unlearned can be given power to "thrash the nations" with such strength that their arms become the Lord's arms in wielding the weapons of truth.

I realize increasingly that we are utterly dependent upon the Lord. Sometimes we make the serious mistake of thinking that we somehow "pay" completely for our own sins through our repentance and that we must become "perfect" through setting goals and achieving them through our own great effort. But if we are honest about it, we learn soon enough that no matter how earnestly we labor, we always fall woefully short. Only the Lord can make full and final compensation for our mistakes and our inadequacies. The good news of the gospel is that he really will do that for those of the broken heart and contrite spirit who do all they can in good-faith.[12] As Nephi said so simply, "For we know that it is by grace that we are saved, after all we can do." (2 Nephi 25:23.)

The other side of this coin, however, is that the Lord *cannot* save us without our own good-faith effort — "all we can do" — no matter how much he would give to make us his. Some people worry about becoming so dependent upon God that they might give up their own agency. But I do not believe God could take away our agency, even if he wanted to. For that reason, I suspect he is far more conscious of our agency than we are. He not only would not, he cannot control us against our will.

William James was right: Despite our dependence on the Lord, whether he can fulfill his promises also depends on us. In that sense, God may need us — and we may need each other — more than we have any idea. So he calls upon "the weak things of the world" and augments their own strength, making their arms into his arms as they "fight manfully" for him.

As we sense how much he needs us in this way, we will see that the more we have to give him, the more it means to him when we give him all we have.

What terrible risks we are taking! Is it possible that the great plan of life would have been frustrated if Adam and Eve had not chosen as they did, or if the Savior had not been willing voluntarily to drink the bitter cup? I suppose the Lord would have found some other way. But insofar as a struggle for *my* soul is part of the war between Good and Evil, if I fail in my part, modest though it may be on a cosmic scale, the war is lost as far as I am concerned.

George Eliot wrote about the famous violin maker, Antonio Stradivari, who correctly understood the relationship between his work and God's: "'Tis God gives skill, but not without men's hand: He could not make Antonio Stradivari's violins without Antonio." And because the master violin maker understood that, he said to himself, "If my hand slacked, I should rob God, since God cannot make a Stradivari violin without Antonio."

We cannot know how much difference our valiance actually makes to the final cosmic outcome in the struggles mankind faces before the real end of history. Our individual part may seem limited and modest; but it is not trivial.

In addition, we may well find that our most important arenas of battle are not in highly visible or even highly ideological settings, but are in a multitude of small-scale circumstances. Leo Tolstoy's sad story of adultery, *Anna Karenina,* eloquently teaches this truth with irrefutable understatement. Indeed, in interesting counterpoint to Fukuyama's question about the "end of history," Tolstoy once said he could "see no reason whatsoever to seek out general laws of history," because the greatest moral struggles occur in prosaic, everyday events.[13]

Russian literature scholar Gary Morson builds on Tolstoy's point: "Most historians and philosophers tend to focus on the big events—on wars, revolutions, [and] dramatic incidents. Individual people, too, tend to [dwell on the meaning of] exceptional events and big decisions."[14]

But "Tolstoy's characters achieve wisdom when they learn not to seek the great and poetic but to appreciate the small and prosaic."[15] Thus, rather than looking for large, visible patterns or waiting for grand moments on the historical stage, the wisest of Tolstoy's characters assume personal responsibility for the integrity of their lives on a routine and ordinary basis, "like the moment-to-moment conscientiousness of a good mother."[16]

For this reason, *Anna Karenina* cautions us powerfully against believing that romantic passion detached from family responsibility is the ultimate form of love. On the contrary, love is nowhere more potent or more significant than in marriage and family life. At the same time, it is hard to "imagine Romeo and Juliet routinely sitting down to breakfast," because even a strong, stable marriage can seem "hopelessly boring and middle class" to those who think life's romance and meaning are found only in grand and dramatic gestures.[17]

This insight reinforces rather than undermines our commitment to lend our strength to God in the historic war between Good and Evil, because that war is being fought on a daily basis, right now, in every personal relationship, in every home, and in every work place. "Most literature and most Western thought has described evil as something grand, terrifying, and Satanic, but Russian literature teaches us that [evil] is ordinary and banal." Thus, the devil who visits Dostoevsky's Ivan Karamazov is "petty, commonplace, fashionably liberal, and politely skeptical. Hell, it turns out, is just like the world—it has adopted the metric system—and the devil himself is, remarkably enough, an agnostic."[18]

In the accumulation of our small-scale choices, our attitudes, our habits, our quiet influence on other individuals or small groups — in the *aggregation* of a thousand moments, here a little and there a little — we are fighting the greatest of wars on the grandest stage of history. Here God must count on our *voluntarily* taking the initiative for what Tolstoy called "moral alertness," *precisely because* the environment seems ordinary and prosaic, with no glaring lights, screaming sirens, or atomic blasts to warn us that there is, in fact, a war going on.

In this environment of subtle, at times almost invisible, warfare, the Lord's dependence on our voluntary action illustrates those "inevitable occasions" William James described, where "inaction ... must count as action, and when not to be for is to be practically against." Here belief becomes a "living attitude, and involve[s] conduct on our part."[19]

The idea that God may benefit from our help is delightfully illustrated by the play, *The Green Pastures,* by Marc Connelly. This play is not to be taken as religious doctrine — including its inference that God has just been making everything up as he goes along. *The Green Pastures* tells the story of man's spiritual history from Adam until the time of Christ from the viewpoint of children in a Christian black culture.

As the play opens, we see a group of children having a fish fry in heaven. When "de Lawd" comes upon the scene and asks, "How's de fish fry goin?" the children are very sad, because they don't have enough "firmament" — which sounds something like custard — to go with the fish. So de Lawd "rares back" and pronounces a miracle, creating enough firmament so they'll never again have to worry about having enough. Then there is so much leftover firmament that he decides to use it to create an earth where some of his "chillun" can live and grow — as something of an experiment.

Then we see the stories of Adam and Eve, Noah and the Flood, and Moses leading the "Chillun of Israel" out of Egypt. Then the people become so wicked that God thinks he should have left no survivors after the Flood; in fact, he repents of ever having created them. They are so bad he decides to just let them self-destruct.

In a scene showing God's "office" in heaven, Abraham, Isaac, Jacob, and Moses come to plead with "de Lawd," urging him to reconsider. But he replies, "Ev'ry day fo' hund'eds of years you boys have come in to ask dat same thing. De answer is still de same!"

But then God is bothered every time a certain man passes his office without coming in. Gabriel (his assistant) tells him that's just old Hosea, a recent prophet: "You needn' be bothered by him hangin' aroun' de office all de time. I'll tell 'im. Who's he think he is?"

At this point, let us introduce Hosea, the Old Testament prophet, by recalling Elder Ronald Poelman's talk in the April 1982 General Conference. Telling the Hosea story in a modern setting, Elder Poelman described a man whose wife left him for an ugly life of adultery and other sins. One day the man saw the woman in a pitiful state and felt such compassion for her that he paid her financial debts and asked her to come home with him, that he might heal her pain. As he did so, he discovered anew his love for her. Elder Poelman compared this man's tender spirit of forgiveness with the mercy Hosea extended to the woman he married, whom the Book of Hosea describes, perhaps allegorically, as "a wife of whoredoms." (Hosea 1:2.)

The Book of Hosea itself begins by showing Jehovah's anger with the children of Israel, whose unfaithfulness toward God is compared to the unfaithfulness of harlots:

"I will not have mercy upon [Israel's] children; for they be the children of whoredoms." (Hosea 2:4–5.) "For the wickedness of their doings I will drive them out of mine house, I will love them no more." (Hosea 9:15.) But by the end of the book, somehow God's heart is softened: "When Israel was a child, then I loved him, and called my son out of Egypt. . . . [T]hey knew not that I healed them. . . . How shall I give thee up, Ephraim? . . . mine heart is turned within me . . . I will not execute the fierceness of mine anger . . . for I am God, and not man; the Holy One in the midst of thee. . . . [F]or there is no saviour beside me. . . . O Israel, thou hast destroyed thyself; but in me is thine help." (Hosea 11:1, 3, 8–9; 13:4, 9.)

Returning to *The Green Pastures,* we find that the story of Hosea implies for Marc Connelly that perhaps Hosea's spirit of forgiveness somehow helps persuade Jehovah to forgive the infidelity of Israel.

For some reason, every time Hosea walks past God's office, God hears the voice of a man on the earth. The man is Hezdrel, one of Hosea's followers, who is preparing to help defend Jerusalem in a great battle. God is tempted to go down to earth to see this man, but, in his frustration with his children's weaknesses, he refuses to go.

Gabriel says, "I hates to see you feelin' like dis, Lawd." God replies, "Dat's all right. Even bein' Gawd ain't a bed of roses." Then Hosea's shadow is seen once more, and God rushes to look out his window at the earth below. "I hear you," he says. "I know yo' fightin' bravely, but I ain't comin' down. Oh, why don' you leave me alone? You know you ain't talkin' to me. *Is* you talkin' to me? I cain't stand yo talkin' dat way." So God decides to go down, not to help, but just because "I'm jest feelin' a little low, an I'm only comin' down to make myself feel a little better, dat's all."

God goes to see Hezdrel, who says, "Who is you?" and God replies, "Me? I'm jest an ol' preacher, from back in de hills. . . . I heard you boys was fightin'. I jest wanted to see how it was goin'."

HEZDREL: Well, it ain't goin' so well.

GOD: Dey got you skeered, huh?

HEZDREL: Look yere, who is you, a spy in my brain? . . . Listen, Preacher, we ain't skeered. We's gonter be killed, but we ain't skeered.

GOD: How is it you is so brave?

HEZDREL: Caize we got faith, dat's why!

GOD: Faith? In who?

HEZDREL: In our dear Lawd God.

GOD: But God say he abandoned ev'one down yere.

HEZDREL: Who say dat? Who dare say dat of de Lawd God of Hosea?

GOD: De God of Hosea?

HEZDREL: How come you so puzzled 'bout de God of Hosea?

GOD: I don' know. Maybe I jest don' hear things. You see, I live 'way back in de hills. . . . Ain't de God of Hosea de same Jehovah dat was de God of Moses?

HEZDREL: (contemptuously) No. Dat ol' God of wrath and vengeance? We have de God dat Hosea preached to us. He's de one God. . . . (reverently) De God of Mercy.

GOD: Hezdrel, don' you think dey must be de same God?

HEZDREL: I don' know. I ain't bothered to think much about it. . . . Dat ol' God, . . . I guess he lived wid man so much dat all he seen was de sins in man. Dat's what made him de God of wrath and vengeance. Co'se he made

91

Hosea. An' Hosea never would a found what mercy was unless dere was a little of it in God, too. Anyway, he ain't a fearsome God no mo'. Hosea showed us dat.

GOD: How you s'pose Hosea found dat mercy?

HEZDREL: De only way he could find it. De only way I found it. De only way anyone kin find it.

GOD: How's dat?

HEZDREL: Through sufferin'.

GOD: (After a pause) What if dey kill you in de mo'nin, Hezdrel?

HEZDREL: If dey do, dey do. Dat's all. . . .

GOD: (Proudly) Dey cain't lick you, kin dey, Hezdrel?

HEZDREL: (Smiling) I know dey cain't. (Trumpet) You better get out o'yere, Preacher. . . . It'll soon be daylight.

GOD: I'm goin'. . . . Want me to take any message?

HEZDREL: Tell de people in de hills dey ain't nobody like de Lawd God of Hosea.

GOD: I will. If dey kill you tomorrow, I'll bet dat God of Hosea'll be waitin' for you.

HEZDREL: I *know* he will.

GOD: (Quietly) Thank you, Hezdrel.

HEZDREL: Fo' what?

GOD: Fo' tellin' me so much. You see, I been so far away, I guess I was jest way behin' de times."

In the next scene, God is in his office with Gabriel, who says, "You look awful pensive, Lawd. You been sittin' yere, lookin' dis way, an awful long time. Is it somethin' serious, Lawd?

GOD: Very serious, Gabriel.

GABRIEL: (Awed by his tone) Lawd, is de time come for me to blow [mah horn]?

GOD: Not yet, Gabriel. I'm just thinkin' . . . bout somethin' de boy tol' me. Somethin' 'bout Hosea, and himself. How dey foun' somethin'.

GABRIEL: What, Lawd?

GOD: Mercy. . . . Through *sufferin'*, he said. . . . I'm tryin' to find it, too. It's awful impo'tant to all de people on my earth. Did he mean dat even God must suffer?"[20]

God looks out over the audience and a look of surprise comes into his face. Then he seems to realize the terrible price he must pay with his own life to find the mercy he seeks. The lights go out, and just before the final curtain falls, a voice offstage cries, "Oh, look at him! Oh, look, dey goin' to make him carry it up dat high hill! Dey goin' to nail him to it! Oh, dat's a terrible burden for one man to carry!"

Even allowing for its doctrinal limitations, this story calls to mind again the Lord's words to Sidney Rigdon: "Wherefore, I call upon the weak things of the world, those who are unlearned and despised, to thrash the nations by the power of my Spirit; And their arm shall be my arm, . . . and they shall fight manfully for me; and their enemies shall be under their feet." (D&C 35:13–14.)

Could it be, even if only in some small way, that "God himself . . . may draw vital strength and increase of very being from our fidelity?"

We know that our Father in Heaven is a God of body, parts, and passions. He is not some cold, abstract essence. When I think of God's passions, I think of how my own passions — my sense of love or sorrow or joy — have much greater depth than they had twenty or thirty years ago. Knowing that, I can only imagine how much deeper his feelings must run.

Do you think the things we do could stir his feelings? I was touched once to hear a college student describe what it meant to her to know that the Savior bears the pain of all her sins. She said that nothing motivated her obedience more than her desire not to make his burden any heavier than it already is.

I have always been moved by Enoch's account of what it was like to see the Lord cry, as He beheld the wickedness of his children who were in the grip of Satan's chains. Enoch was astonished. He recalled God's limitless power and majesty, then he asked, "How is it *thou* canst weep?" The Lord replied, "Behold these thy brethren; they are the workmanship of mine own hands, and I gave unto them their knowledge [and their] . . . agency; And unto thy brethren have I . . . given commandment, that they should love one another, and that they should choose me, their Father; but behold, they are without affection, and they hate their own blood. . . . Satan shall be their father, and misery shall be their doom; . . . wherefore should not the heavens weep, seeing these shall suffer?" (Moses 7:31–33.)

Even though our Father is omnipotent and omniscient, he does feel emotion, and he feels it deeply. Thus, the Almighty God, the Lord of Hosts, wept; for he could not and would not revoke man's agency.

For this very reason, in the approaching showdown in the war between Good and Evil, it does matter to him when we lend our strength to his cause. Being a parent and a teacher helps me understand how that could be, because I have recently come to know the feeling of being lifted and encouraged by my former students or by my own children, who are becoming old enough to see human needs with adult eyes. Similarly, I recently saw a family to whom I helped teach the gospel over twenty-five years ago. Their righteous endurance and their high expectations of me make me yearn to become as faithful as they naturally think their missionary is: Those I once tried to lift now lift me.

Not many years ago, Elder LeGrand Richards, then in his nineties, gave a devotional talk at Ricks College. I sat behind him on the stand holding his cane, which he asked me to tap against the heel of his shoe when he had only two minutes left. As he told his wonderful stories, I saw the tears in the eyes of the students in the first few rows. I still remember one of them later saying that she believed hearing her Father in Heaven talk to his children will surely be much like hearing Elder Richards talk to the Ricks students.

After the devotional, we tried to usher him out of the auditorium to protect his strength, but he stopped us and said firmly, "Aren't you going to let me shake hands with the young people?" We protested that he shouldn't spend his precious strength standing in line to do that, especially because he hadn't eaten anything in several hours. He shook his head and smiled, trying to be patient with us, then said, "Listen, brethren, these young people think I am here to strengthen them, but the main reason I am here is because *they* strengthen *me!* Now you let me shake hands with as many of them as want to come." So he stood in line for more than an hour, and seemed stronger afterward than he was before. Elder Richards literally drew vital strength and increase of being from his association with the faithful Saints.

Elder Marion D. Hanks once said that the most important factor in solving human problems is, very simply, the competence and the character of the people trying to solve them. There is a great need today for even a sprinkling of skilled, intelligent people here and there across the earth, who have also developed some standing with the Almighty through a lifetime of devotion to Him. Having done their best to prepare to help Him in this way, they will be in a position humbly to ask Him to help them, not only with the big problems, but with an endless collection of small problems that together threaten the peace and safety of mankind as never before.

"We are all enlisted," as the LDS hymn says, in what appears to be the final battle between Good and Evil; and here, as "in all important transactions of life," wrote William James, "we have to take a leap in the dark. . . . If we decide to leave the riddles unanswered, that is a choice; if we waver in our answer, that, too, is a choice: but whatever choice we make, we make it at our peril. If a man chooses to turn his back altogether on God and the future, no one can prevent him," not even the Lord himself.[21]

We need him, but he also needs us, to help ensure that life truly can fulfill us with the riches of eternity. Concluded William James:

> These, then, are my last words to you: Be not afraid of life. Believe that life *is* worth living, and *your belief will help create the fact*. The 'scientific proof' that you are right may not be clear before the day of judgment. . . . But the faithful fighters of this hour . . . may then turn to the faint-hearted, who here decline to go on, with words like those with which Henry IV greeted the tardy Crillon after a great victory had been gained: "Hang yourself, brave Crillon! we fought at Arques, and you were not there."[22]

Notes

1. William James, *Essays on Faith and Morals;* ed. Ralph Barton Peery (Cleveland: The World Publishing Company, 1962), pages 53–54.

2. *Essays on Faith and Morals,* page 30.
3. *Essays on Faith and Morals,* pages 23–24.
4. *Essays on Faith and Morals,* page 28. Emphasis added.
5. *Essays on Faith and Morals,* page 28.
6. *Essays on Faith and Morals,* pages 30–31. Emphasis added.
7. Rudyard Kipling, "Recessional, *"One Hundred and One Famous Poems* (Chicago: The Reilly & Lee Co., 1958), page 41.
8. Francis Fukuyama, "The End of History?" *The National Interest* (Summer 1989), page 3.
9. C.S. Lewis, *Mere Christianity* (New York: MacMillan Company, 1943), page 51.
10. Aleksandr Solzhenitsyn, "A World Split Apart," Harvard University Commencement Address, 8 June 1978. Emphasis added.
11. See Ezra Taft Benson, "The Power of the Word," *Ensign* (May 1986), page 79; Joseph Fielding Smith, *Doctrines of Salvation,* 3 vols., comp. Bruce R. McConkie (Salt Lake City: Bookcraft, 1954–56), 3:43.
12. See *The Broken Heart.*
13. See Gary Saul Morson, "Prosaics: An Approach to the Humanities," *The American Scholar* (Autumn 1988), pages 515–518.
14. Morson, "Prosaics," page 519.
15. Morson, "Prosaics," page 519.
16. Morson, "Prosaics," page 523.
17. Morson, "Prosaics," pages 523–524.
18. Morson, "Prosaics," pages 523–524.
19. *Essays on Faith and Morals,* page 24.
20. *Sixteen American Famous Plays,* Bennett A. Cerf and Van H. Cartmell (Garden City, New York: Garden City Publishing Company, 1941), pages 161–70.
21. *Essays on Faith and Morals,* page 62.
22. *Essays on Faith and Morals,* page 31.

CHAPTER SIX

When Do the Angels Come?

God is merciful unto all who believe on his name; therefore he desireth, in the first place, that ye should believe, yea, even on his word. And now, he imparteth his word by angels unto men, yea, not only men but women also.

(Alma 32:22–23.)

At selected moments in history, God has sent his holy angels to instruct, witness, comfort, and minister to his children. Think of the angel who visited Adam after the Fall to teach him about the Atonement; the angel who announced to Mary that she would conceive and bear the child, Jesus; the angels who sang glories to God and declared peace on earth at the moment of Christ's birth; the angel who comforted the Savior in his hour of anguish in the Garden of Gethsemane; the angels at Christ's tomb, who told the two Marys that he was risen; the angels who came to Joseph Smith with the Book of Mormon and the keys of the restored priesthood.

No wonder the angels came at such times. These were the crowning events of human history: the Fall and the first promise of redemption for mankind, the birth of Christ, the completion of the Atonement, the Savior's resurrection, and the restoration of the gospel.

But holy angels have come at other times, moments that were significant not because of their historic grandeur, but because of their personal, spiritual meaning in the lives of ordinary but faithful men and women. Some angelic visitations of this kind were highly visible, even overpoweringly so: think of the angels who ministered to the Nephite children in the sublime account recorded in 3 Nephi 17; the angel who came to chastise Alma the younger and the sons of Mosiah in answer to a father's prayer (see Mosiah 27:11–16); the angel who wrestled with Jacob through the night and changed his name to Israel (see Genesis 32:24–32); or the angel who reproved Laman and Lemuel's treatment of young Nephi (see 1 Nephi 3:29).

There may be some difference between these two kinds of angelic assignments — those who come on official priesthood business and those who come to minister in very personal ways. For example, I have heard some people wonder if angels must always be male. It will not surprise me to learn some day that the angels who visit the earth on special assignments related to priesthood keys were indeed all males, such as the appearance of Moses and Elijah on the Mount of Transfiguration (see Matthew 17:2–3), or the appearances of Moroni or Peter, James and John to restore the Aaronic and Melchizedek Priesthood authority to Joseph Smith. (See D&C 13; 128:20.)

But not all angels must be male, and not all angelic visits are to men. As Alma said, God "imparteth his word by angels unto men, yea, not only men but women also." (Alma 32:23.) Moreover, there may be a difference between "ministering" and "administering" angels. As stated by President Joseph F. Smith,

> When messengers are sent to minister to the inhabitants of this earth, they are not strangers, but from the ranks of our kindred, friends, and fellow-beings and fellow-servants. The ancient prophets who died were those who came to visit their fellow creatures upon the earth. . . . In like manner our fathers and mothers, brothers,

> sisters and friends who have passed away from this earth, having been faithful, and worthy to enjoy these rights and privileges, may have a mission given them to visit their relatives and friends upon the earth again, bringing from the divine Presence messages of love, of warning, or reproof and instruction, to those whom they had learned to love in the flesh.[1]

This chapter is primarily concerned with ministering angels who come for personal reasons. Frequently, angelic visits of this kind are very quiet — sometimes so quiet that those who receive the manifestation are unaware of all that is taking place. This limited awareness should cause no surprise. For reasons bound up in mortality's very purpose, God has deliberately drawn a veil between our world and the world of the angels. That veil involves the root principle of faith: "Faith is things which are hoped for and not seen; wherefore, dispute not because ye see not, for ye receive no witness until after the trial of your faith." (Ether 12:6.)

Yet the ministry of unseen angels remains one of the most sublime forms of interaction between heaven and earth. The angelic presence not only reveals powerful evidence of God's concern for us; the angelic presence, even when unseen, also bestows tangible assurance and spiritual sustenance upon those in great need.

Think, for example, of the angel who came to comfort the sleeping prophet, Elijah, when he was in such despair that he wished to live no longer. (See 1 Kings 19:4–8.) Or recall when Joseph Smith "saw the Twelve Apostles of the Lamb, . . . in foreign lands, standing together in a circle, much fatigued, with their clothes tattered and feet swollen, with their eyes cast downward, and Jesus standing in their midst, and they did not behold Him. The Savior looked upon them and wept."[2] In this same panoramic vision, the Prophet Joseph "saw Elder Brigham Young standing in a strange land, . . . in a desert place, upon a rock in the midst of about a dozen men . . . who appeared hostile. He was preaching in their own tongue, and the angel of God standing above his head, with a drawn sword in his hand, protecting him, but he did not see it."[3]

For an unforgettable picture of the unseen angelic armies that protect God's faithful children, think of Elisha's frightened young servant who cried when he was surrounded by an ominous army, "Alas, my master! how shall we do?" Answered Elisha, "Fear not: for they that be with us are more than they that be with them." Then "Elisha prayed, and said, Lord, I pray thee, open his eyes, that he may see. And the Lord opened the eyes of the young man; and he saw: and, behold, the mountain was full of horses and chariots of fire round about Elisha." (2 Kings 6:15–17.)

Sometimes Church leaders may ask us to accept callings or to assume obligations that strike us as inconvenient or distasteful—or worse. At such times we may feel like saying to ourselves in a tone of irritation, "The Lord will not leave me alone." But at other times, when we, like the young servant, feel overwhelmed and surrounded by enemies and troubles, there comes the comforting assurance: *The Lord will not leave me alone.*

An honest and colorful nineteenth-century Latter-day Saint named Eli H. Pierce preferred that the Lord would leave him alone; then, as he came to know the reality of unseen angels, he discovered the other meaning of not being left alone.

Eli was utterly astonished when his calling as a full-time missionary was announced over the pulpit at the October 1875 General Conference. Prior to that moment, his life "had been entirely given up to temporalities." He didn't know the scriptures, he had made only one attempt at public speaking, and his work for the railroad "would have deprived me of . . . religious services even had my inclinations led in that direction, which I frankly confess they did not." He smoked cigars, played billiards habitually, and wrote that a phrenologist said he was "too level-headed to ever make a sanctimonious church member." Thus, his mission call made him marvel and wonder "if the Church were not running short of missionary material?"

When he received word of his call, Eli Pierce was "sitting lazily thrown back in an office rocking chair . . . reading a novel and . . . sucking a [massive] old Dutch pipe." But immediately upon hearing that he had been called, Eli wrote, "I threw the novel in the wastebasket, the pipe in a corner, and started up town to buy a catechism. Have never read a novel nor smoked a pipe from that hour." He later said the "thought of disregarding the call . . . never once entered my mind." His only concern was, "How can I, who am so shamefully ignorant and untaught in doctrine, do honor to God . . . and merit the trust reposed in me by the Priesthood?"

Some of Eli's friends predicted he "would tire of working for glory before I had been out six months" and would "seek my level by uniting with some comedy troups or minstrel show." But he was rebaptized, set apart as a missionary, and traveled forthwith to New York City.

Brother Pierce labored first in "prayerfulness" and "humility" to develop his own faith, until at last he "obtained the coveted testimony" and was "blessed of the

Lord in freedom of speech." After preaching the gospel for a number of months with considerable success in various eastern states, Eli had an unusual experience in a small branch of the Church in Pennsylvania.

He was asked by the branch president to help administer to the president's youngest child, who was near death. When the child's mother objected to the blessing but would not leave the child's bed, Eli and the father "retired to an upper room to pray." The mother then sent her older little girl "to spy on us." The two men "prayed earnestly and fervently, until we felt that the child would live." Then they noticed the little girl "standing in the half-open door gazing intently into the room," as if she were "entranced for some seconds."

After her father spoke to her, the little girl asked, "Papa, who was that other man in there?" He answered, "Brother Pierce." She said, "No, I mean that *other* man." He replied, "There was no other, darling, except Brother Pierce and myself; we were praying for baby." She shook her head, and, with perfect composure, said, "Oh, yes there was; I saw him standing between you and Mr. Pierce, and *he was all dressed in white.*"

The little girl reported her experience to her mother, "who tried every means in her power to persuade the child that it was a mere delusion, but all to no purpose. . . . She knew what she had seen and nothing could shake that conviction. The baby was speedily restored to perfect health."[4]

When do the angels come? They come for such as this.

President J. Reuben Clark, Jr. eloquently captured the blessing of unseen angels in the lives of ordinary, devoted people in his masterful sermon, "To Them of the Last

Wagon." President Clark delivered this message in 1947 on the one-hundredth anniversary of the entry by Brigham Young and the pioneers into Salt Lake Valley. He expressed thanks for "Brothers Brigham and Heber and Wilford" and the other "mighty men" who led the early Saints across the wild plains. But he paid his primary tribute to the "vast multitude" who settled the valleys of the Great Basin under their leaders' direction, amid "hardship and suffering, neverending work and deep privation, tragic woes and heart-eating griefs, abiding faith and exalting joy," their "testimony burning always like an eternal fire on a holy altar, that the restored gospel was true."[5]

As the title of his talk suggested, President Clark reserved his most reverent gratitude for "the meekest and lowliest" of the pioneer Saints, represented by "the last wagon in each of the long wagon trains" that toiled across the plains and mountain canyons. In possible analogy to the feelings of rank-and-file Church members who may believe they have only limited access to heavenly visions and angelic influences, he compared the last wagon with "the Brethren" who led the wagon trains, "out in front where the air was clear and clean and where they had unbroken vision of the blue vault of heaven."

By contrast, "back in the last wagon, not always could they see the Brethren way out in front, and the blue heaven was often shut out from their sight by heavy, dense clouds of the dust of the earth. . . . Sometimes, they in the last wagon glimpsed . . . the glories of a celestial world, but it seemed so far away, and the vision so quickly vanished, because want and weariness and heartache and sometimes discouragement were always pressing so near." And while the "Saints buoyed up the Brethren out in front with encouragement, with praise, and sometimes even with adulation," those in the last wagon simply "prayed again and pushed on, with little praise, with not too much encouragement, and never with adulation. For there was nearly always something wrong with the last wagon or with its team."

After describing the grinding frustrations of the last wagon, with its lame oxen, broken hubs, and sick children, President Clark spoke of a pregnant mother trying to breathe through heavy, choking dust. Then, at last:

"The morning came when from out of that last wagon floated the la-la of the newborn babe, and mother love made a shrine, and Father bowed in reverence before it. But the train must move on. So out into the dust and dirt the last wagon moved again, swaying and jolting, while Mother eased as best she could each pain-giving jolt so no harm might be done her, that she might be strong to feed the little one, bone of her bone, flesh of her flesh. *Who will dare to say that angels did not cluster round and guard her and ease her rude bed,* for she had given another choice spirit its mortal body, that it might work out its God-given destiny?"

President Clark then concluded: "My mother was one of those babes so born in 1848, ninety-nine years ago."[6]

Thinking of angels watching over this Utah-bound exodus of nineteenth-century Israel brings to mind the Lord's promise to Moses as he prepared to lead Israel out of the wilderness of Sinai: "Behold, I send an Angel before thee, to keep thee in the way, and to bring thee unto the place which I have prepared." (Exodus 23:20.)

This vivid imagery of the ministering of unseen angels in the pioneer era introduces another illustration from Church history that will suggest a more general perspective about when the angels come — a comparison between the dedication of the Kirtland Temple and the dedication of the Nauvoo Temple.

The veil between heaven and earth is fixed enough that even when the angels are there, we are not likely to be immediately aware of their presence. Yet, even in the early stages of our own spiritual development, it is not uncommon for us to experience unmistakable contact with the unseen world. Sometimes these experiences carry sufficient impact to move our sense of belief to a sure sense of knowledge, and we exclaim with Alma, "O then, is not this real?" And Alma replies to us, "Yea, because it is light; and whatsoever is light, is good, because it is *discernible.*" (Alma 32:35; emphasis added.)

Nonetheless, our tasting of this light does not yield perfect knowledge, for we must patiently nourish the tree "that it may get root" against the day "when the heat of the sun cometh and scorcheth it." (Alma 32:37–38.) As we wait for additional flashes of spiritual light, our days of nourishment and testing can last many years.

The early manifestations of "discernible" light in our spiritual development frequently occur in youthful conversion experiences, missionary service, or perhaps attendance at a Church-owned university, college, or Institute of Religion. These crucial, formative periods of spiritual breakthrough may be compared with the Kirtland period in Church history; and the years that follow may be compared with the period of Nauvoo and beyond.

The early years of Kirtland were an unusually happy time for Joseph Smith and the Saints. A steady stream of wonderful events had blessed them all in only a few years: the vision in the grove, the publication of the Book of Mormon, the formal organization of the Church, the optimistic launching of missionary work, the school of the prophets, and mighty revelations outlining the glorious future that awaited the Saints of the Most High. It was a youthful, buoyant time. The Saints had no inkling of what awaited them, coiled like a deadly snake barely around the corner of history: mobs, persecution, apostasy, and martyrdom.

One of Joseph Smith's biographers described a winter in the happy Kirtland years: "It was a season for snug fires, jolly company, and rewarding study. . . . Joseph attended several weddings and officiated at several others, enjoying the festivities. . . . As he wrote, 'Our hearts were made glad with the fruit of the vine . . . and we felt disposed to patronize all the institutions of heaven.' Parties and feasts were frequent, and Joseph was 'much blessed with company' at home. . . . [He] enjoyed the out of doors, also, and frequently noted in his journal that the weather was perfect for sleighing."[7]

And then the angels came. Indeed, the dedication of the Kirtland Temple in March of 1836 represented what might be the greatest spiritual outpouring in all of modern Church history. Joseph wrote in his journal that, shortly after the dedicatory prayer was offered, "Frederick G. Williams arose and testified that [during the prayer] an angel entered the window and took his seat between Father Smith and himself. David Whitmer also saw angels in the house."

In a special evening meeting, the Prophet wrote that "Brother George A. Smith arose and began to prophesy, when a noise was heard like the sound of a rushing mighty wind, which filled the Temple, and all the congregation simultaneously arose, being moved upon by an invisible power; many began to speak in tongues and prophesy; . . .

and I beheld that the Temple was filled with angels. . . . The people of the neighborhood came running together (hearing an unusual sound within, and seeing a bright light like a pillar of fire resting upon the Temple), and were astonished at what was taking place." At one of the concluding meetings, Joseph wrote, "The Savior made his appearance to some, while angels ministered to others, and it was a Pentacost and an endowment indeed, long to be remembered, for the sound shall go forth from this place into all the world, and occurrences of this day shall be handed down upon the pages of sacred history, to all generations."[8]

Now contrast those glorious experiences with the dreadful conditions under which the Nauvoo Temple was dedicated less than ten years later. Joseph and Hyrum had been slain. The Church was racked with dissension and apostasy, and the dark spirit of the martyrdom hovered over Nauvoo like the destroying angel of death. The Saints knew they could not stay. They worked frantically to finish the temple, even as they also hurried to gather provisions and prepare wagons for their plunge into the great westward unknown: "Although they knew that they would have to give it up, their temple was to be the finest they could produce. The work went on despite poverty, anxiety, sickness, and desperate efforts to prepare for the exodus. Toward the last, when harassments increased, laborers carried their weapons with their tools and worked under constant guard. They built an edifice of beautiful white sandstone, towering over the countryside and visible for miles up and down the Mississippi."[9]

Part of the Nauvoo Temple was dedicated in October 1845, even before it was finished; and in December of that year, Brigham Young began to administer the temple ordinances day and night. Within a mere two months, the first company of wagons started across the frozen Mississippi, never to return. Within three years, the temple was burned by an arsonist, and two years later a tornado demolished what was left of it.

The story is told of a blind convert named Brother Williams who came from Massachusetts to Nauvoo in time to help complete the temple. The other workmen wondered how to use him, but they finally assigned him to turn the grindstone in the carpenter shop on the temple site. Brother Williams had heard the stories of Kirtland, and he believed fervently that when the Nauvoo Temple was dedicated, the Savior and even the resurrected Joseph would return. He anticipated great spiritual manifestations that would heal his blindness. He believed that each stone they were laying brought him one step closer to the Savior's healing hand.

But the Nauvoo Temple dedication was no Kirtland. As far as we know, there were no visible manifestations, no angelic ministries, no Pentacost.

Our youthful years as missionaries and students are, despite their typical growing pains, frequently a kind of Kirtland for us: a simple and beautiful time, filled with intellectual breakthroughs, private spiritual moments, and emerging idealistic convictions often reinforced by living in a complete community of Saints. Those years may lift us for a time above the noise and smoke and confusion of worldly valleys to a high mountain peak, where the air is fresh and pure, where our vision is clear and unbroken, and where we can develop a growing closeness to the Infinite.

But the day always seems to come when we must leave our Kirtlands. When we do, sooner or later, we may experience our own kind of Nauvoo, perhaps more than once. We will have our own frozen rivers and parched deserts to cross, a moral or financial or intellectual wilderness to tame. It will not always be fun. Perhaps we will feel bewildered and disappointed, and we may look back longingly to those youthful years, wondering why we cannot recapture the way things were in our days of Kirtland.

When our Nauvoo comes, some of us may feel like Joseph who was sold into Egypt. Rather than finding ourselves buoyed up by the broad-scale support system of Kirtland's Mormon village, we may live in the lonely isolation Joseph knew among the Egyptians. But we, like Joseph, must bloom where we are planted, no matter what corner of the vineyard we inhabit. Of course we, like Joseph, will not be *of* the world, even as we remain *in* the world, that it may be said of us as it was of him: he was "a goodly person, and well favored." (Genesis 39:6.)

Amid such loneliness, we will be pressured to follow the moral norms of a spiritually alien culture. We must then be like Joseph, who, when tempted by Potiphar's wife, "fled, and got him out." (Genesis 39:12.) The Potiphars who observe us may then say of us, as was said of Joseph, that "the Lord was with [him]," making "all that he did to prosper in his hand." (Genesis 39:1– 3.) And eventually they may say, as Pharaoh said of Joseph, "Can we find such a one as this is, a man in whom the Spirit of God is?" (Genesis 41:38.) Then, as Elder Neal A. Maxwell once said, when we are surrounded by worldly famines of the soul, we, like Joseph, must help to find solutions, not just be another hungry mouth to feed.

After leaving our Kirtland, we may find ourselves living

in a culture that offers little reinforcement for our belief in the ideals of family life. The surrounding environment may even discourage and attack our devotion to marriage and children. Some of us may then begin to feel a growing sense of distance in our marriages, as those around us take for granted that modern men and women should not feel bound by unconditional family commitments. But we will know better, for we lived once in Kirtland, where the spirit whispered to us that the doctrine is true: marriage is sacred and love is forever.

When our Nauvoo comes, some of us may feel the waning of our sense of *spiritual* wonder, as the accumulating pressures and pollutions of life seem to cast doubt on the reality of inspiration or the worth of the institutional Church or the value of giving ourselves unselfishly to others. Especially in that kind of Nauvoo, some of us may turn away bitterly and say that the stories of Kirtland are not really true. "How could they be true?" some will ask. "We see no angels here, not now, when we need them most. What happened at Kirtland must have been the foolish imagination of our youth." We will feel pressure to see things this way, for we may be surrounded by unbelievers who whisper tauntingly in our ears as did the enemy in Nauvoo: "Your Prophet is dead. Wake up — it was all a childhood dream."

When our Nauvoo comes, it will neither surprise us nor throw us off course, if we have kept the image of Kirtland burning brightly in our memories. When our Nauvoo comes, "It is all right," we will say, "we understand. We receive our full witness only after the trial of our faith. After much tribulation cometh the blessings." And we will pick up our wagons and our families and head West.

113

As we do, we will sense that Kirtland was given to us as a first witness, to be told to our children and their children's children, that they may know that God is the Lord. As Felix Mendelssohn wrote in *Elijah*, "He, watching over Israel, slumbers not nor sleepeth." We will *know* that, always, for we were there, that season in the Mormon village of Kirtland. Yet we also understand the profound reasons why the Nauvoos must come.

I still think of Brother Williams, his blind eyes glistening with hope, waiting for Jesus and his angels to come to the Nauvoo Temple. I don't know what happened to him after Nauvoo. Did he find the healing he hungered for? Did he find his Savior and see the face of Brother Joseph? I suppose that he and the other faithful ones of Nauvoo *did* find the enlightenment and the peace they sought—but later, perhaps within the last wagon along some dreary prairie trail, or in struggling to build a new life, far away in the West.

I suppose that Brother Williams made the same discovery as did the Saints in the Martin and Willie handcart companies, when many perished as they were trapped by heavy, early snows on their way across the plains. Elder James E. Faust once quoted from one of the survivors of that handcart tragedy:

> Not one of that company ever apostatized or left the Church, because every one of us came through with the absolute knowledge that God lives, *for we became acquainted with him in our extremities.* I have pulled my handcart when I was so weak and weary from illness and hunger that I could hardly put one foot ahead of the other. I have gone on [to some point I thought I could never reach, only to feel that]

114

the cart began pushing me. *I have looked back many times to see who was pushing my cart, but my eyes saw no one. I knew then that the angels of God were there.*[10]

Such *unseen* angelic manifestations in the "extremities" of our lives may, over time, have more profound meaning than the more visible outpourings of Kirtland. If we are true and faithful, the Lord himself may be "in [our] midst and [we] cannot see [him]." (D&C 38:7.) Even if we do not see him, he can "be on [our] right hand and on [our] left, and [his] Spirit shall be in [our] hearts," and the angels who came to Kirtland will be "round about [us], to bear [us] up." (D&C 84:88.)

Moreover, our memories of Kirtland can be enriched by our later, perhaps more turbulent, experience. The very meaning of earlier witnesses may well grow richer with the perspective of time. It is because of what we saw in Kirtland that we ventured to Nauvoo. That we have once seen so clearly is our witness that we can again see clearly, with greater depth, even in the very midst of our afflictions.

After all, the angels *are* there. And someday, perhaps not so far away in time or space, we might be prepared enough and have reason enough at last to see the angels of Kirtland once more. The conditions on which our vision may pierce the veil are not fully known to us. Those conditions are not always known even to the prophets. When Elijah was about to be taken from the earth, his successor as prophet to Israel, Elisha, asked that a double portion of Elijah's spirit might remain with him. Elijah said this was "a hard thing; nevertheless, if thou see me when I am taken from thee, it shall be so unto thee; but if not, it shall not be so." Suddenly, flaming horses and a

115

chariot of fire appeared and took Elijah by a whirlwind into heaven. And the Lord granted the desire of Elisha's heart, for his eyesight pierced the veil: "And Elisha saw [the angels], and he cried, My father, my father, the chariot of Israel and the horsemen thereof." (2 Kings 2:9–12.)

Who are those horsemen? When do they come, and where do they go?

They must not be far away, for they have come again in the modern age. Not long before the dedication of the Kirtland Temple, Joseph Smith's scribe saw "in a vision, the armies of heaven protecting the Saints in their return to Zion."[11] The next day, after Joseph and the Twelve had sealed holy anointings on the heads of one another, "the heavens were opened unto Elder Sylvester Smith, and he, leaping up, exclaimed: 'The horsemen of Israel and the chariots thereof.' "[12]

Whoever they are, in their chariots of fire, the horsemen of Israel watch over the Saints with such care and power that we know of a surety: "They that be with us are more than they that be with them." (2 Kings 6:16.)

From Eli Pierce and J. Reuben Clark, Jr., I learn that the angels can be very near at the blessing of a sick child or at a baby's birth. From the history of Kirtland, I learn that they come to celebrate and bear unforgettable witness in the formation of faith, even if we must wait for more complete witnesses until our faith has been tried by fire. From the scriptures, I learn that God's angels can ever bear us up, whether we see them or not. Knowing this, I suppose that the angels come in our hours of greatest personal need. A moment of high spiritual significance in one person's life may not seem to have cosmic or historic meaning, but such moments can have acute personal consequences that matter very much to those who are sent to strengthen us from beyond the veil.

When do the angels come? I suppose they come:

When a father who feels unworthy to bless his child asks another man to speak for God to his little one; and the father, listening, resolves that he will become worthy, that the priesthood for his children may be his own hands and his own voice.

When a young woman is with a young man whom she honestly loves, but he grows weak in the face of temptation. In the crucial moment, she teaches him tenderly about restraint, and he knows that she truly cares for him, and that she cares for his future and her own, and perhaps one day for their future together.

When a man in his midthirties is tormented by a crisis of his faith in the restored Church—he sees a close friend lose his testimony and leave the Church; his bishop uses poor judgment in handling an unfounded accusation against the man's wife; and he finds that the sermons and lessons he hears in Church seem increasingly superficial. He suppresses his impulses toward cynicism and cries out in many prayers for perspective, patience, and new light.

When a mother and her child watch together after dark, as the moon comes up to greet them, and they talk together softly of the secrets of the night, of the God above who loves them, and the purpose of all they see. The seeds of faith are planted and love's own warmth is felt.

When a father walks the floor of a hospital room through the hours of the night, trying to comfort the cries of a very sick baby, knowing that the sleep he needs must wait, perhaps for many nights; and knowing that the life of his child is in the Lord's own hands.

When a kindly bishop befriends the young, showing

that he understands them and can keep their secrets. And in the quiet of the evening one comes to him to talk; and as one heart listens to another, the tears of remorse flow together with the tears of understanding. A soul begins to heal, forgiveness begins to work its miracle, and the bishop has a lifelong friend.

When a husband speaks harsh words that wound his companion's heart; seeing her tears of pain, this time his anger turns to shame and he asks her to forgive. She forgives him, again, but asks if such hurt must come again; and not only does he promise, but next time controls that anxious tongue, and this temple marriage becomes gradually more celestial.

When a single woman blessed with both intelligence and professional training feels continually undervalued and put down by many men with whom she interacts at Church and with whom she works at her office. Years of frustration build toward anger that begins to color her interpretation of every event and every relationship. She remembers the blessing of having been close to sensitive, loving patriarchs in her life—her father, a teacher, and a humble stake patriarch—and she prays for patience and the gift of knowing how to help both men and women work in harmony together with compassionate understanding.

When a tall, college-age grandson has far too much to do, but sees, without being asked to see, that his frail grandmother yearns to be taken for a walk outdoors. He knows his needs can wait, and he engages her fully in happy conversation as they stride along together, his strong arm holding her clasped hands.

I suppose the angels come for such as this.

Notes

1. *Joseph F. Smith, Gospel Doctrine* (Salt Lake City: Deseret Book Co, 1949), pages 435–36.
2. Joseph Smith, *History of The Church of Jesus Christ of Latter-day Saints,* 7 vols., ed. B. H. Roberts (Salt Lake City: The Church of Jesus Christ of Latter-day Saints, 1932–51), 2:381.
3. *History of the Church,* 2:381.
4. See Eliza R. Snow, *Biography and Family Record of Lorenzo Snow* (Salt Lake City: Deseret News Company Printers, 1884), pages 407–13.
5. J. Reuben Clark, Jr., "To Them of the Last Wagon," reprinted in *The New Era* (July 1975), page 8.
6. "To Them of the Last Wagon," pages 10-11.
7. Donna Hill, *Joseph Smith: The First Mormon* (Garden City, New York: Doubleday & Company, Inc., 1977), page 194.
8. *History of the Church, 2:427–33.*
9. *Joseph Smith: The First Mormon,* page 435.
10. As quoted in James E. Faust, "The Refiner's Fire," *Ensign* (May 1979), page 53. Emphasis added.
11. *History of the Church,* 2:381.
12. *History of the Church,* 2:383.

Index

121

About the Author

Bruce C. Hafen was sustained to the First Quorum of the Seventy of The Church of Jesus Christ of Latter-day Saints on April 6, 1996. He was formerly Provost of Brigham Young University and Professor of Law at BYU's J. Reuben Clark Law School. A graduate of Dixie College, BYU, and the University of Utah Law School, he has served as Director of Research and Evaluation for the Correlation Department of the Church, as President of Ricks College, and as Dean of the BYU Law School. In the Church, he has served as a Gospel Doctrine teacher, as a counselor in a bishopric and in a stake presidency, and as a Regional Representative. He is a nationally recognized authority on family law and education law. His numerous articles appear in the *Ensign, Brigham Young Magazine,* and such professional legal journals as *Harvard Law Review* and the *American Bar Association Journal.*

He and his wife, Marie K. Hafen, have seven children and ten grandchildren. Their home is in Orem, Utah.